Kings, Deliverers, and Prophets in Luke's Journey Narrative

Kings, Deliverers, and Prophets in Luke's Journey Narrative

DENNIS W. CHADWICK

WIPF & STOCK · Eugene, Oregon

KINGS, DELIVERERS, AND PROPHETS IN LUKE'S JOURNEY NARRATIVE

Copyright © 2022 Dennis W. Chadwick. All rights reserved. Except for brief quotations in critical publications or reviews, no part of this book may be reproduced in any manner without prior written permission from the publisher. Write: Permissions, Wipf and Stock Publishers, 199 W. 8th Ave., Suite 3, Eugene, OR 97401.

Wipf & Stock
An Imprint of Wipf and Stock Publishers
199 W. 8th Ave., Suite 3
Eugene, OR 97401

www.wipfandstock.com

PAPERBACK ISBN: 978-1-6667-3240-5
HARDCOVER ISBN: 978-1-6667-2607-7
EBOOK ISBN: 978-1-6667-2608-4

03/29/22

New Testament Scripture quotations contained herein are from the New Revised Standard Version Bible, copyright, 1989, by the Division of Christian Education of the National Council of the Churches of Christ in the U.S.A. Used by permission. All rights reserved.

Old Testament Scripture quotations contained herein, unless otherwise noted, are from the Lexham English Septuagint, second edition (LES), copyright 2019 Faithlife, LLC (DBA Lexham Press) and are used by permission. All rights reserved.

Contents

Preface		vii
Acknowledgments		ix
1	Entering In	1
2	Luke's Reflections of King David's Odyssey	7
3	Luke's Imitation of Moses as Deliverer	32
4	Luke's Parallels of Judges as Deliverers	52
5	Luke's Echoes of the Prophets Elijah and Elisha	70
6	The Purpose of Luke's Journey Narrative	96

Appendix 1: The Roles of Luke 13:31–35   103
Appendix 2: Richard Hays and *Echoes of Scripture in the Gospels*   105
Bibliography   109

Preface

SOME READERS OF THIS book will have also read my previous book, *Both Here and There: Studies in Concentric Parallelism in the Gospel of Luke*. If you are one of them, you deserve an explanation for discrepancies between the two books. In *Both Here and There* I devoted a chapter to "Jesus' Journey and David's Progress" and wrote an appendix on "Jesus' Journey and Elijah's Journey," both of which I also cover in this book, but differently than before.

It seemed very appropriate in *Both Here and There* to adopt a kingdom of God hermeneutic for textual connections I observed between the Lukan journey and David's progress toward Israel's throne. Weren't both Jesus and David kings of Israel, the past great king and the eschatological king? Wouldn't Jesus have much to say, directly or indirectly, about King David? But after my first book, as I traced back newly observed intertextual ties between the Lukan journey and David's story, it became less and less likely that kingdom of God ethics and theology was the primary thread joining them together.

I needed to account for echoes in Luke that tied back to non-kingly voices and events in the David story, voices like those of Ahimelech, Jonathan, Abigail, Achish of Gath, the medium of Endor, and Abner. The interpretive approach that might hold together all of these threads seemed to be something like reading the Lukan journey as a loose Greco-Roman imitation of David's story.

After finishing the first book, however, I observed more and more intertextual ties of the same sort between the Lukan journey and the Elijah/Elisha story. What is more, the same appeared to be true even of ties between Luke and the books of Numbers and Judges! How could ten chapters of Luke tie back concurrently to many, many chapters of four OT books? A new hermeneutic was needed, but Greco-Roman imitation wouldn't do. (See chapter 6.) What seemed to answer the question was accepting Luke's journey narrative as a unique literary creation that connected to OT texts in its own idiosyncratic way by means of persistent reflections or echoes.

Thus *Kings, Deliverers, and Prophets* comes to different conclusions than *Both Here and There* about the meaning of Luke 9:51—19:44. I hold firmly, however, to the chiastic analysis of Luke's journey narrative presented in the earlier book. I hope return readers will find the current book's conclusions, compared to the former book's, more theologically satisfying and provocative.

Acknowledgments

I AM GRATEFUL TO Kevin Lee, who was at the time of our collaboration a graduate student at the University of Kansas. For many months two decades ago, Kevin studied with me, comparing NT narrative to OT narrative, although we finally came to a seemingly unfruitful stop in our searches. That fruit did mature, but slowly, following gradual changes in assumptions about intertextual connections.

Much more recently, George Stulac read a draft of this manuscript with rigor, proposing key improvements and needed corrections. And as always, my wife, Judy, did painstaking reading of the manuscript and championed a tone that invites lay readers to discover the riches of scripture with us. And finally, I thank my editor, Brian Palmer, and the rest of the publishing team at Wipf & Stock for their patient and professional shepherding of this author and his text.

> They placed the Chest of God on a brand-new oxcart ... David ... brought up the Chest of God ... celebrating extravagantly all the way.
>
> 2 SAM 6:3, 12 (*MSG*)

> 'You'll find a colt tethered, one that has never been ridden' ....
> They helped Jesus get on.
> As he rode, the people gave him a grand welcome.
>
> LUKE 19:30, 35–37 (*MSG*)

1
Entering In

THE BEST-KNOWN PARABLES OF Jesus are The Good Samaritan and The Prodigal Son. These parables (along with several other strong contenders for best-known) appear *only* in Luke's Gospel, and do not appear in the other canonical Gospels. The same is true of iconic encounters in Luke that Jesus had with his dinner hosts, Martha and Zacchaeus.

These famous Gospel episodes reside within just the middle chapters of the Third Gospel, in a well-defined section of the story that narrates the journey of Jesus and his disciples from Galilee to Jerusalem (Luke 9:51—19:44). Luke's journey narrative holds the *only occurrence in any of the Gospels* of nine parables, three healings, three other life-changing encounters, two discourses, and one lament.[1]

---

1. Parables of Jesus occurring only in Luke's journey narrative (9:51—19:44) include The Good Samaritan (10:27–37), The Begging Friend (11:5–8), The Rich Fool (12:16–21), The Lost Coin (15:8–10), The Prodigal and His Brother (15:11–32), The Dishonest Manager (16:1–9), The Rich Man and Lazarus (16:19–31), and The Unjust Judge (18:1–8). Only in Luke do we find the healings of The Crippled Woman (13:10–17), of The Man with Dropsy (14:1–6), and of The Ten Lepers (17:11–19). Three uniquely Lukan encounters include The Hospitality of Mary and Martha (10:38–42), The Pharisees'

The same journey in Matthew's Gospel boasts only seventy-four verses of text, making up a little over two chapters (19:1—21:11). Mark describes the journey in sixty-three verses, mostly in one chapter of his Gospel (10:1—11:11). Matthew and Mark write approximately the same account of the journey.[2] Luke unfolds his journey narrative in 424 verses (about ten chapters), telling a story that ends like the others do, but which otherwise is a mostly different and much longer story. *Luke shapes the journey story uniquely and expansively, quite unlike Matthew's or Mark's telling.*

And it is not simply that Luke is a more exacting storyteller when it comes to the journey to Jerusalem. If anything, Matthew and Mark propel their accounts forward more effectively than Luke does. Luke provides episode after episode, chapter after chapter, describing no discernable movement down the road, and often with little or no discernable sequence of any other kind between episodes. In his journey narrative, *Luke is up to something that has little relationship to movement on the landscape or the passage of time.*

Luke tells Theophilus (1:1-4) that the narrative is "orderly, *kathexēs*" (1:3). The evangelist once uses the word "orderly" elsewhere to mean a series of places along a route (Acts 18:23), but the narrative in Luke 9:51—19:44 does not offer such an itinerary. Yes, the journey narrative begins and ends with a few episodes following a route, but 80 percent of the narrative offers little movement. Overall order in 9:51—19:44 must be another sort of order.

Luke reports Peter using the word "orderly" as Peter recalls for his listeners the sequence in time of God's prophets (Acts 3:24). But in Luke's narration of the journey, transitions between reported episodes rarely emphasize one event following another in an explicitly progressive sequence of time, especially in that middle 80

Warning (13:31-33), and Zacchaeus' Dinner Party (19:1-10). One can read a discourse on Humility and Hospitality only in Luke 14:7-14 and a discourse on Unprofitable Servants only in Luke 17:7-10. Finally, only Luke describes when Jesus Weeps over Jerusalem (19:41-44). Sectional titles above, where available, are taken from or adapted from the NRSV.

2. In his Gospel, John implies multiple trips for Jesus to Jerusalem. John does not narrate a climactic singular journey of Jesus from Galilee to Jerusalem.

percent. *Collective order in the Lukan journey is an order of neither time nor place.*

While the story of Jesus in the remainder of Luke's narrative unfolds in sequences of time and place, Luke invests the journey portion with different order, a kind of literary order. *Luke 9:51— 19:44 systematically echoes stories of God's great Old Testament (OT) servants.* This book explores structured echoes of the OT in Luke's journey narrative.

We will explore an echoed relationship between Luke's journey narrative and the OT books of Numbers, Judges, 1–2 Samuel, and 1–2 Kings. We will examine how Luke 9:51—19:44, by this means, confirms texts earlier in Luke that proclaim Jesus as the eschatological deliverer, as the eschatological king, and as the eschatological prophet. Luke does so by compiling and editing a unique Galilee-to-Jerusalem journey narrative in which Jesus' acts and words echo those of Moses (from Sinai to the Jordan) and the Judges, echo David's odyssey to the throne, and echo the ministries of Elijah, Elisha, and other prophets to the Northern Kingdom of Israel.[3]

In some of the journey narrative's episodes, Luke echoes only one of his three OT models.[4] Most often Luke finds something similar among two or all three models that can be echoed by a teaching of Jesus or by an event in Jesus' life. OT features echoed in the Lukan journey include themes, plot elements, quantities, and locations, as well as the personal tendencies or moods or inclinations or manners of particular people.[5]

To echo episodes in three OT models, the evangelist turns to the oral and written Jesus tradition, as he says in Luke 1:1–4.

3. Luke's OT model for Moses comes from the book of Numbers.

4. By his editorial choices in compiling the journey narrative, Luke evidently assumes that Moses' story from Sinai onward and the book of Judges together are a singular model of God's deliverance from opponents.

5. These are only a few examples of the multiple and sometimes unexpected ways that Luke acknowledges OT texts, and based on them, organizes his journey narrative. When Luke's OT models describe disbelief in God or opposition to God's rule, Luke sometimes (but not always) parallels by countering with a Gospel episode that can be seen to critique or correct the OT character(s). See in chapter 6 on "Commentary."

He gathers parables, teachings, sayings, axioms of Jesus, and encounters with Jesus that echo themes, plots, and characters in the models. In this remarkable process, Luke assembles and edits Jesus episodes that often concurrently echo features of three models.

For the practical demands of description in this book, I borrow terms used to describe Greco-Roman literary imitation, even though Luke does not engage in Greco-Roman literary imitation as he assembles and edits the journey narrative in his Gospel. The terms I borrow are those that modern critics employ in describing how one ancient author imitates another ancient author. For our purposes, themes or words of six OT books may serve as models for specific themes and words in Luke's journey narrative. Accordingly, certain themes and words in the Third Gospel approximate or parallel themes or words from OT narratives. I supplement these formal terms by everyday terms such as "echo" and "reflect."

Some of Luke's literate readers, possibly Theophilus (1:1–4), knew a literary imitation on sight. Higher education, as a basic practice, trained all writers and aspiring authors to imitate the respected masters. Students across the Greco-Roman world, by incessant copying, memorization, recitation, and restructuring exercises, became intimately familiar with a canon of key works produced by old masters.[6] Theophilus, or other literate, first-century Christians (very few though they were) might see and feel any literary pulses of imitation in Luke's journey narrative. But not a single comment along that line exists among Luke's first interpreters!

Nor do other early interpreters notice any sustained parallel between Luke's presentation of Jesus' journey and the great OT leaders, prophets, or kings, let alone a sustained concurrent parallel. Neither the apostolic fathers, the Greek fathers, nor the Latin fathers interpret the journey in this manner. And for that matter, neither does any interpreter of Luke from then until now. In this book we make an unprecedented set of observations and interpretive claim.

Our approach makes a reasonable assumption that Luke read and quoted the OT from a Greek (Septuagint) OT. In Luke's day

---

6. See Dupertuis, "Writing and Imitation," 3–8.

ENTERING IN

there were a few Greek translations of the OT, translated from a few variants of the Hebrew OT. All these Greek OT texts were generally called the Septuagint (LXX), and they differed from Hebrew texts only in minor details.[7]

Luke reflected parts of six LXX books in 9:51—19:44 of his Gospel. We document that Lukan activity, using the New Revised Standard Version (NRSV) for the text of Luke, and the Lexham English Septuagint (LES) for texts from the six OT books.[8] Standard English Bibles translated from OT Hebrew offer essentially the same narrative as does a translation from OT Greek. Accordingly, our readers can easily follow most of this study in their Hebrew-based English translations by simply looking up the analogous chapters and verses. Any chapter or verse numbering differences between the LXX and Hebrew-based translations will be clarified as needed.

Luke systematically connects Jesus' journey (9:51—19:44) to David's odyssey (1 Kgdms 19:11—2 Kgdms 6:23). We catalog these connections in chapter 2, treating David first because the intertextual connections between model and reflection are frequently quite transparent and because the LXX model is comparatively compact.

Second, Jesus' journey in Luke parallels God's deliverers (Moses and the Judges) in more than forty chapters of OT narrative (Num 10–36; Judg 1–21), texts seen by Luke as one extended sequence. We catalogue these parallels in chapters 3 and 4.

Third, Jesus' journey in Luke resounds with echoes of Elijah and Elisha in 3 Kingdoms 19:1—4 Kingdoms 17:24. We note these echoes in chapter 5. Finally, chapter 6 considers what kind of an innovation Luke has accomplished in his journey narrative.

Figure 1 illustrates the analysis we describe in chapters 2–5.

7. Jobes and Silva, *Invitation to the Septuagint*, 13–14.

8. Any italics within quotations from the NRSV or LES are mine, given for emphasis. Any parenthetical statements included in quotations are mine, given to clarify OT/NT echoes. The familiar English titles 1–2 Samuel (Sam) and 1–2 Kings (Kgs) are in the LXX replaced by 1–4 Kingdoms (Kgdms). Thus 1 Sam is 1 Kgdms, and 1 Kgs is 3 Kgdms. Occasionally we bring forward significant Greek correspondences between the LXX and Luke, transliterating from the Tischendorf LXX text in the *NIV Triglot Old Testament* and from *Novum Testamentum Graece* 27.

Kings, Deliverers, and Prophets in Luke's Journey Narrative

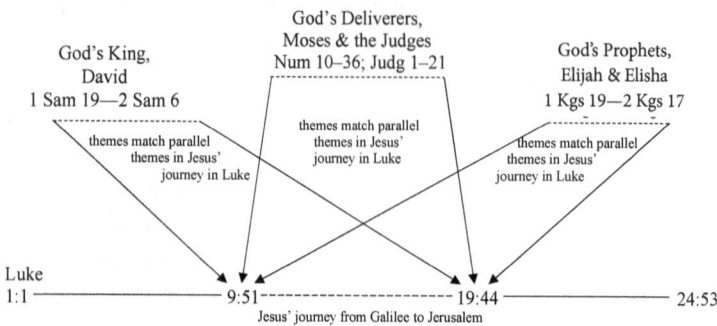

Figure 1: Analysis

For some, Figure 1 may raise a question of logic or mathematics: if three OT narratives parallel the same Lukan narrative, should not the three OT narratives parallel one another? The answer in this case is no. The term "parallel" must be understood more precisely. Only certain words and themes of each OT narrative correspond to certain words and themes of the Lukan narrative. *A subset* of 1 Samuel 19—2 Samuel 6 corresponds to *a subset* of Luke 9:51—19:44; *a subset* of Numbers 10-36 and Judges 1-21 corresponds to *a partially different subset* of Luke 9:51—19:44; and *a subset* of 1 Kings 19—2 Kings 17 corresponds to *yet another, partially different, subset* of Luke 9:51—19:44. My analysis of connections between three OT narratives and the journey narrative in Luke implies no compositional parallels between the three OT narratives. Luke sees that David, Moses/Judges, and Elijah/Elisha have in common key leadership roles under the purposes of God. As great as these were (king, deliverers, prophets), the Great One has come, ushering in the day of God.

First, then, we turn to Jesus' journey as it reflects David and his odyssey.

> So right there, while they were looking at him, he pretended to go crazy, pounding his head on the city gate and foaming at the mouth, spit dripping from his beard.
>
> 1 SAM 21:13 (*MSG*)

> "Black magic," they said. "Some devil trick he's pulled from his sleeve."
>
> LUKE 11:14 (*MSG*)

2

Luke's Reflections of King David's Odyssey

A MODERN INTERPRETER AGREES that Luke's story of Jesus' journey builds on the story of King David. N. T. Wright argues that

> David's story progresses through his life as an outcast, leading a motley crew of followers in the Judean wilderness, and reaches its initial climax at the moment when Saul and Jonathan are slain and he, David, is anointed king over Israel. And one of his first acts is to go to Jerusalem to take the city as his capital. Jesus' story progresses through his wandering with his motley followers in Galilee and elsewhere, and reaches its initial climax when he comes to Jerusalem amid expectations that now at last Israel's god was to become king.[1]

Although Wright does not provide chapter and verse boundaries from the story of David or from the Gospel, David's story that Wright describes must extend from about 1 Samuel 16 to about 2 Samuel 5. Likewise, the parallel in Luke apparently covers from 9:51 to some point in Luke 19. As to the nature of the NT/OT

---

1. Wright, *New Testament and the People*, 379.

relationship of these stories, Wright speaks of David being a type of Jesus the Messiah, and of King Jesus being a fulfilment of King David.[2]

Wright observes, as we do, a parallel between the vagabond years of David and the Lukan journey of Jesus to Jerusalem.[3] We detect, however, that Luke assembled episodes from the gospel tradition (making up 9:51—19:44) to reflect words and themes, particularly of 1 Samuel 19:11—2 Samuel 6:23. And Luke saw his model primarily in a Greek OT, rather than in a Hebrew OT. Thus, Luke's reflections of David in the journey narrative arise from 1 Kingdoms 19:11—2 Kingdoms 6:23.

DISTINCT THEMATIC REFLECTIONS

Readers can detect in David's story distinct thematic parallels between 1-2 Kingdoms and Luke that occur *in the same order*. Here are selected examples of features from both model and reflection appearing in their twin sequence:

1-2 Kgdms	Luke
David asks Ahimelech for five sacred loaves from the tabernacle. The priest gives the loaves. David also asks for the sword of Goliath. The priest gives it to David (1 Kgdms 21:1-11a).	A man in a parable pleads, "Lend me three loaves..." The neighbor gives the loaves. Further, the Father gives the Holy Spirit to those who ask (11:5-13).
Saul seeks an informer (22:6-8).	An evil generation seeks a sign (11:29-30).
Nabal is a rich fool who will not share his feast. God ends Nabal's life suddenly (25:2-17).	A parable's rich fool wants to hoard and consume his produce. God takes the fool's life suddenly (12:13-21).

    2. Wright, *New Testament and the People*, 381. Yuzuru Miura considers Wright's argument to be weak due to lack of credible and specific evidence (*David in Luke-Acts*, 6), but Miura nevertheless thinks that Wright is generally on the right track (*David in Luke-Acts*, 221).

    3. David is mentioned in only one episode of the journey narrative: 18:35-43.

Luke's Reflections of King David's Odyssey

David asks a cast-out, "Where are you from?" The cast-out had not eaten bread nor drunk water for the three days since his master left him behind (30:11–13).	A former host says, "I do not know where you come from." His former guests, wanting back in, object that in the past "we ate and drank with you . . ." Jesus warns listeners lest they be thrown out of the kingdom of God (13:25–28).
David sent shares of spoils of war to towns in many parts of Judah (30:21–25).	"People will come from east and west, from north and south, and will eat in the kingdom of God" (13:29).
David, living in border country, asks the Lord, "Should I go up to one of the cities of Judah?" The Lord answers, "Go up" (2 Kgdms 2:1).	"Friend, move up higher" (14:10).
Abner says to Ishbosheth, King Saul's heir, I will "remove the kingdom from the house of Saul," and "erect the throne of David for Israel . . ." (2 Kgdms 3:1–11).	When a master declares, "You cannot be my manager any longer," the servant frets, "My master is taking the position away from me" (16:1–9).
"Evil men have murdered a righteous man . . ." (4:11).	"He must endure much suffering and be rejected by this generation" (17:25).
David's sons and daughters (5:13–16).	"Let the children come to me." "It is to such as these that the kingdom of God belongs" (18:15–17).
They loaded the ark of the Lord onto a new cart (6:1–5).	Jesus rode on a colt on which no one had ever yet sat (19:28–44).

There are many more such reflections, *all occurring in parallel order in the two narratives*. We provide below extensive tables of reflections from 1–2 Kingdoms in Luke. Persistent thematic parallels between 1 Kingdoms 19:11—2 Kingdoms 6:23 and Luke 9:51—19:44, from start to finish of both narratives, mark out Luke's journey narrative as a reflection of the OT narrative.

ARTISTIC REFLECTION

In addition to assembling texts to thematically reflect David's story, Luke also arranges an artistic feature in the journey to reflect an artistic feature in David's story. Chiasm may not be easily recognizable to modern readers, but ancient readers living in a culture of Greek sensibilities would consider it normal and beautiful for chiasm to appear in all types of literature. Chiasm was not only beautiful, but also didactic in that the central statement of the form provided an interpretive prompt.

Luke introduces 11:33–36a as a chiastic structure reflecting a chiastic structure in 1 Kingdoms 23:1–13, appearing *in the same sequential location* in both narratives.[4] In 1 Kingdoms, eleven plot developments align in five thematic pairs, the first episode aligning with the last, the second episode with the penultimate one, and so on.[5] In the center stands a single reminder that David now has access to the priestly ephod of Abiathar, a means of inquiring of the Lord for specific guidance.[6]

> First Kgdms 23:1 *And it was reported to David*, saying, "Look, the foreigners are attacking at Keilah, and they are plundering it; they are trampling the threshing floor."
>
> > 2 And *David inquired of the Lord*, saying, "Should I go and strike these foreigners?" *And the Lord said*, "Go, and you will strike down these foreigners and you shall strike Keilah."
> >
> > > 3 And the men of David said to him, "Look! *We, here in Judah, are afraid. What will happen if we go* to Keilah and join the spoils of the foreigners?"

---

4. First Kgdms 23:1–13 below lacks verse 12 of the Hebrew Bible. Codex Alexandrinus lacks the verse, thus it was left out by Swete in his *Old Testament in Greek*, 593, and consequently left out by the editors of the LES.

5. Italics in the chiastic structure are mine. They are intended to highlight alignments of content.

6. Tsumura points out that in 1 Kgdms 23:11–12 David inquires chiastically: ABCDED'C'B'A' (Tsumura, *First book of Samuel*, 555). Multiple chiasms commonly occur in close proximity. Readers who see one chiasm could well look closely at the context for additional ones.

4 And so David set to inquire yet again of the Lord, and the Lord answered him and said to him, "*Rise and go down* to Keilah because *I have given the foreigners into your hand.*"

5 And so David and the men went with him to Keilah and fought with the foreigners, and they fled from their face, and he led away their livestock, and he struck a great blow against them. And David saved the people who dwell in Keilah.

6 And it happened that with the fleeing of Abiathar son of Ahimelech to David, that he went down with David to Keilah with the ephod in his hand.

7 And it was reported to Saul that David was in Keilah, and Saul said, "*God sold him into my hands* since he has trapped himself by going into a city with doors and bars." 8 So Saul *summoned all the people for battle to go down* to Keilah, to confine David and the men with him.

9 And David learned that *Saul was not quietly ignoring the evil against him.*

And so David said to Abiathar the priest, "*Bring the ephod of the Lord.*" 10 And David said, "*Lord, God of Israel*, with my ears, your servant has heard that Saul seeks to come against Keilah, to destroy the city because of me. 11 Will it be a trap? And now will Saul come down just as your servant heard? Lord God of Israel, tell your servant." And the Lord said, "It will be a trap."

13 And David rose, and there were about four hundred men with him. And they departed from Keilah and went wherever they went. And to Saul, *it was reported that David had escaped* from Keilah, and he stopped the expedition.

The unknown author of the Keilah account displaced verse 6 from strict chronological order to provide this verse as the literary and theological hub of a chiasm, thus turning the episode into a discourse as well as a story. Thirteen verses express not only the story of David and Keilah, but also foreshadow kingship and priesthood joined effectively within the confines of a town. First Kingdoms 23:6 is not a curiously misplaced plot element; rather, it is the center and main point of a chiastic discourse (or teaching).[7]

---

7. Thus there is no reason to consider verse 6 a textual corruption.

In a textual place in Luke corresponding to 1 Kingdoms 23:1–13, Luke appropriates parabolic teachings from the Jesus tradition that were already shaped, or could be shaped, as a chiasm.[8] In Luke's imitation we find a chiasm not containing turns of plot but containing entwined sayings of Jesus, in eight lines, two of them forming a center:

Luke 11:33 "No one after *lighting a lamp*

> puts it *in a cellar*, but on the lampstand so that those who enter may *see the light*.
>
> > 34 Your eye is *the lamp of your body*.
> >
> > > *If your eye is healthy, your whole body is full of light;*
> > >
> > > *but if it is not healthy, your body is full of darkness.*
> >
> > 35 Therefore consider whether the *light in you is not darkness*.
> >
> > 36 If then your whole body is full of light, with no part of it *in darkness*, it will be as *full of light*
>
> as when *a lamp gives you light with its rays.*"

Thus we see that chiastically entwined sayings of Jesus reflect a chiastic form in the parallel episode in 1 Kingdoms.[9]

Artistic Lukan composition reflects artistic LXX composition. Themes in the Lukan journey reflect themes in David's odyssey. With that preparation of our vision, let us explore the reflections in detail. I urge readers of this book to have ready before them an Old Testament turned to 1 Kingdoms (1 Sam) 19:1—2 Kingdoms (2 Samuel) 6:23, and a New Testament turned to Luke 9:51—19:44, in order to explore both stories in parallel while reading the rest of our chapter 2.

---

8. This is one of two of Luke's journey episodes that has the ring of John's Gospel, thus stylistically standing out on that account also (see also 10:21–22).

9. Luke 11:33–36 could possibly be taken as a Lukan commentary on David and Saul, but more likely, Luke's whole reflective strategy makes one general point about Jesus and David.

LUKE'S REFLECTIONS OF 1 KINGDOMS 19:1 – 2 KINGDOMS 6:23 IN LUKE 9:51 – 19:44

As explained further in Appendix 1, Luke 13:31-33 and 34-35 serve both as essential middle blocks of journey text *and* as journey bookend texts. As a bookend text, Luke 13:31-33 connects to the beginning of Jesus' journey. The verses can be read as the nonlinear *beginning of the beginning of the journey*, in addition to the place the text occupies in the linear order of the journey.[10] Luke's reflection of OT text begins at 13:31-33, and then continues in 9:51-56.

1 Kgdms 19:11-18, imitated by Luke 13:31-33 and 9:51-56

"And it happened in that night..." (19:11).	"At that very hour..." (13:31).
David "departed and fled and was saved" (12).	"Get away from here..." (31).
Saul intends "to kill (David) in the morning" (11).	"...for Herod wants to kill you" (31).
"Saul sent messengers to watch him" (11).	"Some Pharisees came" to warn Jesus about Herod's intentions (31).
"Protect your own life this night" (11).	"Get away from here..." (31).
"Tomorrow you will be killed" (11).	"Today and tomorrow, and on the third day" (32); "Today, and tomorrow, and the next day" (33).
Michal resisted Saul and his men by a deception (12-17).	"They did not receive him" (9:53).
Michal faked David's body by putting a household idol "on the bed" (*epi tēs klinēs*) and putting a goat liver "on its head" (*pros kephalēs autou*) (13).	"The Son of Man has nowhere to lay his head" (*tēn kephalēn klinē*. (58).
"David and Samuel went and stayed in Naioth in Rama" (18).	"They went on to another village" (56).

---

10. See Appendix 1.

Kings, Deliverers, and Prophets in Luke's Journey Narrative

1 Kgdms 19:19-24, reflected by Luke 9:57—10:5

"Saul sent messengers to capture David" (19:20).	"Go and proclaim the kingdom of God" (9:60).
"He sent other (*heterous*) messengers" (21).	"The Lord appointed seventy others (*heterous*)" (10:1).
"Saul continued to send messengers a third time" (21).	"Ask the Lord of the harvest to send out laborers into his harvest" (10:2).
Saul was "prophesying" (23).	"Proclaim the kingdom of God" (9:60).
Saul "took off his clothing . . . and fell naked . . ." (24).	"Carry no purse, no bag, no sandals" (10:4).

1 Kgdms 20:1-42, represented by Luke 10:5-42

In Hebrew manuscripts, 1 Samuel 20:16 begins a new sentence of narration: "And Jonathan made a covenant with the house of David, saying, 'May the Lord take vengeance on the enemies of David'" (NRSV). First Kingdoms 20:16 (LXX), however, continues the words of Jonathan's oath to David. There Jonathan adds, ". . . that the name of Jonathan be found from the house of David, and may the Lord seek out enemies for David." As shown in the table below, Luke imitates *not the Hebrew version, but the Greek version* (LXX) of the verse, with its concern about the name of Jonathan.[11]

My/your "father" (20:1, 2 [2x], 3, 6, 8, 9, 10).	"Father" (10:21 [2x], 22 [3x]).
"My father" tells me everything. "Why would my father hide this matter?" (2).	"No one knows . . . who the Father is except the Son and anyone to whom the Son chooses to reveal him" (22).
"If he says this, 'Good,' then there is peace . . ." (7).	"First say, 'Peace to this house!' And if anyone is there who shares in peace, your peace will rest on that person" (5-6).
". . . but if he answers you harshly . . ." (7).	"But if not, it will return to you" (6).

---

11. The RSV renders the LXX and not the Hebrew form of 1 Sam 20:16.

Luke's Reflections of King David's Odyssey

"... you can be sure that evil has been determined by him" (7).	"Yet know this: the kingdom of God has come near" (11).
"It shall be to your cities" (9, LXX only).	Woes on named cities (12–15).
"That the name of Jonathan should be found from the house of David" (16, see the comment prior to this table).	"Your names are written in heaven" (20).
David was to watch from a hidden position (19).	"You have hidden these things..." (21).
A lad was to retrieve practice arrows without knowing the real significance of the shooting (20–22).	"... and have revealed them to infants" (21).
David's place was "noticeable" (25) and "noticed" (27) by King Saul.	"Kings desired to see what you see" (24).
"Because all the days that the son of Jesse should be alive on the earth, your kingdom will not be prepared" (31). Saul insists that Jonathan kill David (31).	"What must I do to inherit eternal life?" (25).
"Saul raised his spear against Jonathan to kill him" (33).	Robbers attacked, "leaving him half dead" (30).
Scene: Jonathan commands (36–38), a boy hurries to do Jonathan's bidding (38), and David sits and listens in hiding (35, 41).	*Scene*: Jesus is Lord (39, 40, 41), Martha busily arranges hospitality for the Lord (40–41), and Mary sits next to Jesus and listens to him (39).
"Hurry quickly and do not stand still" (38).	"Martha, you are worried and distracted by many things" (41).
"The Lord will be a witness between (us) for eternity" (42).	Mary's part "will not be taken away from her" (42).

1 Kgdms 21:1–11, rendered by Luke 11:1–13

In 1 Kingdoms 21, verse numbers differ by one from the same account in the Hebrew Bible. Subtracting one from 1 Kingdoms verse numbers obtains 1 Samuel verse numbers.

"There are from your hand five bread loaves, so give to my hand whatever you find" (21:3).	"Lend me three loaves of bread" (11:5).
David's men may not have these loaves, unless "the servants are kept from a woman" (5).	The friend does not give the loaves, because "the door has already been locked and my children are with me in bed" (7).
The priest gave him the loaves (7).	"He will get up and give him whatever he needs" (8).
"Give (the sword) to me." The priest gave him the sword (10–11).	"The heavenly Father (will) give the Holy Spirit to those who ask him!" (13).

1 Kgdms 21:12–16, countered by Luke 11:14–23

A man able to speak pretends that he is mute: "David set the words in his heart" (21:13).	"The one who had been mute spoke" (11:14).
King Achish rejects David as a madman (15).	Jesus supposedly "casts out demons by Beelzebul, the ruler of demons" (15).
David is a military threat (11–12).	"When one stronger than he attacks him and overpowers him" (22).
"This man will not come into the house" (15).	"A strong man . . . guards his castle" (21).

1 Kgdms 22:1–5, matched by Luke 11:24–28

The Gospel writer sometimes arranges reflections that do not necessarily maintain parallels of protagonist to protagonist and antagonist to antagonist. In 1 Kingdoms 22:1–5 (the following table), David is a chastened protagonist. Arrival at the cave signals for David the end of arranging his own escape from Saul and beginning to trust in God's protection. Luke 11:24–26, however, parallels cave-dwelling David with an unclean spirit. The parallel is not a commentary on David, comparing him to a satanic spirit, but instead the parallel serves Luke's project of broadly associating the story of King Jesus with the story of King David.

Luke's Reflections of King David's Odyssey

"David departed from there and escaped..." (22:1).	"When the unclean spirit has gone out..." (11:24).
...and he went to the cave that is in Adullam" (22:1).	"...it wanders through waterless regions looking for a resting place" (11:24).
"His brothers and the house of his father heard, and they went down to him there" (1).	"I will return to my house from which I came" (24).
The distressed, the debtors, and "everyone afflicted in spirit" went down to him (2).	It brings "seven other spirits more evil than itself, and they enter and live there" (26).
David became leader over about 400 men (2).	"It goes and brings seven other spirits" (26).
David seeks safety for his mother and father (3-4).	"Blessed is the womb that bore you and breasts that nursed you" (27).
God's prophet told David to leave the cave and enter Judah (5).	"Blessed rather are those who hear the word of God..." (28).
So David left and settled in a city of Judah (5).	"...and obey it!" (28).

1 Kgdms 22:6-23, echoed by Luke 11:29-32

In the Scriptures cited in this table, the OT king asks for a sign and the NT public asks for a sign. David was seen and identified (1 Kgdms); Jesus is given as a sign to be perceived (Luke). Saul asserts judgment on a city of priests (1 Kgdms), while in Luke eminent authorities will judge those not responding to the Son of Man. Finally, Saul condemns priests to death (1 Kgdms), but in Luke foreign authorities will issue an undefined condemnation. The Gospel writer thus assembles Gospel texts that are loosely analogous to 1 Kingdoms texts, but he is not concerned to maintain role-to-role parallels (for example, the king wants a sign, but Jesus is a sign). Luke's project requires only that there be identifiable and continuing thematic parallels between David's odyssey and Jesus' journey.

Saul berates his officials and soldiers for their silence about Jonathan's support of David. Saul wants them to be his informers (22:7–8).	"This generation is an evil generation; it asks for a sign" (11:29).
Doeg has recognized David and his men when they obtained supplies from the priest (9–10).	Son of Man is given as a sign to this generation (30).
Saul charges the priests of Nob with conspiracy against the king (13).	The queen of the South and Ninevites will judge this generation (31–32).
"You will die" (16).	They will condemn this generation (31–32).

1 Kgdms 23:1–13, reflected by Luke 11:33–36

Scriptures in this table receive a more detailed analysis on pages 10–12.

David inquired of the Lord through Abiathar's ephod regarding Keilah (23:2, 4, 10–11).	One puts a lighted lamp on a stand so that those who enter may see (11:33).
Through circumstances seeming to benefit Saul's intent to kill David, Saul inferred God's approval of the murder (7).	"Consider whether the light in you is not darkness" (35).

1 Kgdms 23:14–28, countered by Luke 11:37–54

Parallels in this table exhibit further kinds of matches that Luke makes between Gospel text to OT text. Unwashed physical hands implied in the Lukan account match metaphorical hands in 1 Kingdoms. Desire for social notoriety in a synagogue (Luke) echoes a desire for recognition as a lieutenant in David's future kingdom (1 Kgdms). In Luke, a guild of lawyers frustrates the honest faith of common people, while in 1 Kingdoms, town elders betray a small band of refugees.

Luke's Reflections of King David's Odyssey

"The Lord did not hand (David) over to (Saul)" (14). Jonathan "strengthened (David's) hand in the Lord" (16).	The Lord did not first wash (his hands) before dinner (38).
"I will be with you as second" (17).	"You love to have the seat of honor in the synagogues" (43).
Ziphites exposed the location of David's refugee band to Saul (19) and urged Saul to attack the refugees (20).	Lawyers "load people with burdens hard to bear" and do not help to bear them (46).
Ziphites hinder (19–24a).	Lawyers "hindered those who were entering" (52).
Saul pursued David, encamping against him to "catch" him (25–26).	Scribes and Pharisees pressed Jesus hard, "lying in wait for him, to catch him" (53–54).

1 Kgdms 24:1—25:1, imitated by Luke 12:1-12

Verse numbers in 1 Kingdoms 24 differ by one from 1 Samuel 24. Subtract one from 1 Kingdoms verse numbers to find the parallel 1 Samuel verses.

Saul took "three thousand chosen men . . . to seek David" (24:3).	"The crowd gathered by the thousands . . ." (12:1).
Saul went into the cave to relieve himself while David and his men were sitting in the inner part of the cave (4).	". . . so that they trampled on one another" (12:1).
David "cut a flap from Saul's cloak secretly" (5).	"Nothing is covered up that will not be uncovered, and nothing secret that will not become known" (2).
David comes out of hiding in the cave, does face-down obeisance to Saul, his pursuer, and boldly begins speaking to him (9–16).	"Do not fear those who kill the body" (4).

Kings, Deliverers, and Prophets in Luke's Journey Narrative

"I will not lay my hand on my master because he is the Lord's anointed" (11). "May the Lord judge between me and you, and may the Lord avenge me from you" (13).	"Fear him who . . . has authority to cast into hell" (5).
"After whom do you go out . . . ? After a dead dog, and after a single flea?" (15).	"Are not five sparrows sold for two pennies? Yet not one of them is forgotten in God's sight" (6).
"May the Lord be as judge and jury between" us and "may the Lord see and judge" my cause "and acquit me out of your hand" (16).	"Everyone who acknowledges me before others, the Son of Man will also acknowledge before . . . God" (8; see 9–10).
David trusts his life to God when surprising Saul, only making a speech as a defense (1–23).	When they bring you before the rulers, "do not worry about how you are to defend yourselves or what you are to say, for the Holy Spirit will teach you at that very hour what you ought to say" (11–12).

1 Kgdms 25:2–44 imitated by Luke 12:13–38

For most of these imitations, themes (not details) imitate themes (not details).

A man had "three thousand sheep and a thousand goats" (25:2).	"The land of a rich man produced abundantly" (12:16).
He did not share his feast with refugee neighbors (10–11).	He hoarded his wealth, intending to consume it himself (19).
"Nabal is his name, and foolishness is with him" (25).	"You fool!" (20).
"The Lord struck down Nabal, and he died" (38).	"This very night your life is being demanded of you" (20).
Abigail offers food for David and his men (27). "David received . . . everything that she brought for him" (35).	"Do not worry about . . . what you will eat" (22).

Luke's Reflections of King David's Odyssey

King Saul confesses regarding David, "And it will be that the Lord will do to my master every good thing that he has spoken about you. He will charge you to be the ruler over Israel" (30).

"It is your Father's good pleasure to give you the kingdom" (32).

David took "her to himself as his wife" (39). "And David took Ahinoam from Israel, and both of them were wives to him" (43).

A master is about "to return from the wedding banquet" (36).

"Your servant is like a servant girl to wash the feet of your servants" (41). "She followed the servants of David, and she became his wife" (42).

"Blessed are those slaves" (37).

1 Kgdms 26:1–25, matched by Luke 12:39–53

"David rose secretly and went" into Saul's camp (26:5).

"If the owner of the house had known at what hour the thief was coming, he would not have let his house be broken into" (12:39). "The Son of Man is coming at an unexpected hour" (40). "The master . . . will come . . . at an hour that he does not know" (46).

"There was Abner son of Ner, his commander, and Saul was sleeping in a covered chariot, and the people were camping in a circle around him" (5).

Blessed are wakeful slaves when the master comes in the second or third watch (38).

"Why don't you (Abner) take care of your master, the king? For someone came in from the people to destroy the king, your master. It is not good, this thing that you have done. . . . You are sons of execution, who guard our lord king, your master, the anointed one of the Lord" (15–16).

Who is "the faithful and prudent" trusted manager (42)? "The master . . . will cut (the failed slave) in pieces, and put him with the unfaithful" (46).

Saul asks, "Is this your voice, child, David?" (17).

"They will be divided: father against son and son against father" (53).

Kings, Deliverers, and Prophets in Luke's Journey Narrative

1 Kgdms 27:1—28:3a, countered by Luke 12:54—13:9

"It is not good for me unless I am delivered in the land of the foreigners" (27:1).	"Why do you not know how to interpret the present time?" (12:56).
Achish of Gath, a predator to Israel (27:2).	Pilate, a predator to Galileans (13:1).
Better to live in a country town than in the royal city (27:6).	It is no worse to be an unrepentant sinner in Siloam than an unrepentant sinner in Jerusalem (4).
King Achish expects David to raid on the king's behalf. "Against whom did you attack today?" (27:10).	"A man . . . came looking for fruit" (6).

1 Kgdms 28:3b-25, reflected by Luke 13:10-17

In 1 Kingdoms, a woman ministers to the king, whereas in Luke, King Jesus ministers to a woman. The parallels of detail are not comprehensive (they never are), nor do they need to be for Luke to make it clear that Jesus' journey story generally reflects David's odyssey.

A woman was still an active medium in the land (28:3, 7–14, 21–22).	A woman had a crippling spirit (13:11).
Saul fell on the ground without strength (20).	She was bent over and could not stand up straight (11).
Samuel was indignant at being called from the dead (15).	The leader of the synagogue was indignant because Jesus cured on the Sabbath (14).
"I will set before you a morsel of bread, and you should eat, and strength will be in you that you might go on your way" (22). She prepared meat and cakes and fed him (24–25).	"You are set free from your ailment." "He laid his hands on her" (12–13).
Saul rose and went away (25).	"Immediately she stood up straight" (13).

Luke's Reflections of King David's Odyssey

1 Kgdms 29:1—30:25, echoed by Luke 13:18-30

Satraps (kings) look over their troops (29:2).	"What is the kingdom of God like?" (13:18).
Upon seeing alien troops in their military column, Philistine satraps want to know, "Who are these who pass by?" (3).	Some unknown person sows "a mustard seed" in a vegetable garden (19). The resultant plant is obviously different from the garden's crop.
There are potential dire consequences in letting David and his men remain in the troops (3-5).	The mustard plant grows into a huge bush, using up water and nutrients, and providing shelter to potential raiders of the garden produce (19).
"He had not eaten bread and had not drank (sic) water" (30:12).	"We ate and drank with you" (26).
"Where are you from?" (13).	"I do not know where you come from" (25, 27).
"My master" (13, 15).	"The owner of the house" (25).
"My master left me behind" (13).	". . . and you yourselves thrown out" (28).
David sent some of the spoils of battle to Bethel, Ramah, Jattir, Aroer, Ammadi, Siphmoth, Eshtemoa, Gath, Kinan, Saphek, Thimath, Racal, Hormah, Borashan, Athach, Hebron, "all the places that David travelled" (26-30).	"People will come from east and west, and from north and south, and will eat in the kingdom of God" (29).

1 Kgdms 31:1—2 Kgdms 1:27, imitated by Luke 13:31-35

In battle with Israel, Philistines press in to engage Saul and his sons (31:2). Saul is wounded in the abdomen (3) and dies (6). An Amalekite later claims, "I stood over (Saul) and killed him" (1:10).	"Get away from here, for Herod wants to kill you" (13:31).
"On that day" (31:6); "the next day" (31:8); "on the third day" (1:2).	"Today and tomorrow, and on the third day"; "today, tomorrow, and the next day" (32-33).

Kings, Deliverers, and Prophets in Luke's Journey Narrative

David laments the deaths of King Saul and of David's friend Jonathan (1:17–27).	Jesus laments the coming demise of Jerusalem (34–35).

2 Kgdms 2:1–7, imitated by Luke 14:1–24

"Should I go up?" (2:1); "Where shall I go?" (1); "David went up" (2).	"Friend, move up higher" (14:10).
"And now may the Lord show you compassion and truth, and I, indeed, will do this good thing for you" (6).	"You will be blessed because they cannot repay you, for you will be repaid at the resurrection of the righteous" (14).
"David sent messengers to the leaders of Jabesh Gilead" (5), hoping to bring them under David's kingship (7).	"Someone gave a great dinner and invited many" (16).

2 Kgdms 2:8–16, reflected by Luke 14:25–35

Abner and his men went out to do battle with Joab and his men (2:12).	"What king, going out to wage war against another king, . . ." (14:31).
"These men stayed (sat) at the spring of Gibeon on this side and these other men (sat) at the spring in the other side" (13).	". . . will not sit down first and consider" (14:31).
Combatants representing Benjamin and combatants representing David (15).	"My disciple" (26, 27, 33).
Men arose to fight (15).	Whoever "comes to me and does not hate . . . even life itself" cannot be Jesus' disciple (26).
They died together (16).	"Whoever does not carry the cross and follow me cannot be my disciple" (27).

2 Kgdms 2:17–32, countered by Luke 15:1–32

"Three sons of Zeruiah" were there. (2:18; see 3:39: "too cruel for me").	"This fellow welcomes sinners and eats with them" (15:2).

Luke's Reflections of King David's Odyssey

Asahel was the youngest son of Zeruiah (2:18).	The younger son (12–13).
"Swift on his feet as one gazelle in a field" (18).	A man loses one sheep in the wilderness (4).
Asahel determinedly pursues Abner (19). Abner assumes that Asahel is primarily intent on plundering an opponent's armor (21).	A woman searches carefully for one silver coin (8).
"Return" from battle (27, 28, 30).	"I will get up and go" (18). "He set off and went" (20).
"Joab, your brother" (22). "Our brothers" (26). "The people would still be chasing his brother" (27).	"Your brother has come" (27).
Asahel fell and died (23).	"This brother of yours was dead and has come to life" (32).

2 Kgdms 3:1–39, reflected by Luke 16:1—17:10

"I . . . did not rebel" against "the house of David" (3:8).	"If you have not been faithful with what belongs to another . . ." (16:12).
I will "remove the kingdom from the house of Saul" (10).	"You cannot be my manager any longer" (2). "My master is taking the position away from me" (3). "When I am dismissed as manager . . ." (4).
"Restore to me my wife Michal" (14).	"Anyone who divorces his wife and marries another commits adultery, and whoever marries a woman divorced from her husband commits adultery" (18).
"You sought David to be king over you. And now you must act because the Lord has spoken concerning David, saying, 'By the hand of my servant David I will deliver Israel from the hand'" of the Philistines "'and from the hand of all his enemies'" (17–18).	"The good news of the kingdom of God is proclaimed" (16). "Everyone tries to enter it by force" (16).

"May (the guilt) come down on the head of Joab and on all his father's house and may" the house of Joab always face life-threatening crises (29).	"Father, I beg you to send him to my father's house—for I have five brothers—that he may warn them, so that they will not also come into this place of torment" (27-28).
"All the people came to invite David to the funeral meal" (35).	You would say, "Prepare supper for me, put on your apron and serve me" (17:8).
"All the people knew as well as all Israel in that day" that not David, but Joab, put Abner to death (37).	"Occasions for stumbling are bound to come, but woe to anyone by whom they come" (1).

2 Kgdms 4:1—5:5, rendered by Luke 17:11-37

Mephibosheth and "all the men of Israel" (4:1).	Ten persons . . . (17:12).
They grew "weak" and "faint" (1).	. . . suffering from leprosy (17:12).
The narrator provides background on Beeroth, a town on the border between Benjamin and Ephraim (3).	The Lukan narrator comments: "On the way to Jerusalem Jesus was going through the region between Samaria and Galilee" (11).
The original Beerothites fled to Philistia and became resident aliens (3).	"Except this foreigner . . ." (18).
"He fell and became lame. And his name was Mephibosheth" (4).	"He prostrated himself at Jesus' feet" in gratitude. "And he was a Samaritan" (16).
"Here is the head of Mephibosheth son of Saul, your enemy who was seeking your life. And the Lord has given the lord the king vengeance against his enemies as this day . . ." (8).	"The kingdom of God is not coming with things that can be observed; nor will they say, 'Look, here it is!' or 'There it is!'" (20-21).
"Evil men have murdered a righteous man" (11). David's men "killed them and cut off their hands and their feet and hung them by the spring in Hebron" (12).	"But first he must endure much suffering and be rejected by this generation" (25).

Luke's Reflections of King David's Odyssey

"You will shepherd my people Israel, and you will be the one who leads over Israel" (5:2). "He became king and he ruled forty years" (5:4).

Rechab and Baanah beheaded Mephibosheth and carried the severed head to David (4:5–8).

"For, in fact, the kingdom of God is among you" (21).

"Where the corpse is, there the vultures will gather" (37).

2 Kgdms 5:6–16, echoed by Luke 18:1–17

The narrator lists various other names of Jebus: Jerusalem, Zion, city of David (5:6–7).

The Jebusites do not fear David's attack: "David will not come in here" (6).

"David captured the stronghold of Zion" (7).

Attack the Jebusites, "those who hate the soul of David" (8).

"His kingdom was raised up for his people Israel" (12).

"There were for David still more sons and daughters" (13). There are here twenty-four named children (14–15, LXX) born to "wives and concubines at Jerusalem" (13).

"In a certain city . . ." (18:2).

". . . there was a judge who neither feared God nor had respect for people" (18:2).

"She may . . . wear me out by continually coming" (5).

"I am not like other people: thieves, rogues, adulterers, or even like this tax collector" (11).

"All who exalt themselves will be humbled, but all who humble themselves will be exalted" (14).

"Let the little children come to me, and do not stop them; for it is to such as these that the kingdom of God belongs" (16).

2 Kgdms 5:17–25, reflected by Luke 18:18–34

Philistines "went up (to Jerusalem) to seek David" (5:17).

David begins to enjoy life as king of Israel, but the Philistines do not want a unified monarchy in these hills, so they mount an attack against David (17).

"See, we are going up to Jerusalem" (18:31).

"How hard it is . . . to enter the kingdom of God" (24; see 26–27).

27

Kings, Deliverers, and Prophets in Luke's Journey Narrative

David compares the success of his victory to the ease of cutting through water (20).	Jesus compares the difficulty of entering the kingdom to a camel passing through the eye of a needle (25).
"There they abandoned their gods . . ." (21).	"Sell all that you own and distribute the money to the poor, . . ."
". . . and David and the men with him took them" (21).	". . . then come, follow me" (22).
"David did just as the Lord commanded to him . . ." (25).	"Peter said, 'Look, we have left our homes and followed you'" (28, see 29–30).
". . . and he struck down (the Philistines) from Gibeon to the land of Gezer" (25).	"Everything that is written about the Son of Man by the prophets will be accomplished . . ." (31).

The next three Lukan episodes (18:35–43; 19:1–10, 11–27) exhibit Luke's dense reflection of a single brief model text in 2 Kingdoms 6.

2 Kgdms 6:1–5, imitated by Luke 18:35–43

"David and the sons of Israel," proceeding in front of the ark, "were dancing before the Lord with tuned instruments with strength and with songs" and with lyres, stringed instruments, tambourines, cymbals, and flutes (6:5).	A blind man "heard a (noisy) crowd going by" (18:36). "He shouted, 'Jesus, Son of David'" (38). "He shouted even more loudly, 'Son of David'" (39).
"The Lord Almighty who is seated before the cherubim" (2), refers to the gold lid of the ark and its cherubim. God's mercy for the people was sought there by the priest on the Day of Atonement (Exod 25:16–21).	"Have mercy on me!" (38, 39).

2 Kgdms 6:10–12, imitated by Luke 19:1–10

Along the route lived "Obed-Edom, a Gittite" (6:10).	On the way through Jericho, Zacchaeus, a wealthy tax collector, was among the onlookers (19:2–3).

28

David turned the ark "aside to the house of Obed-Edom the Gittite. And the ark stayed in the house . . . three months" (10–11).	"Zacchaeus, . . . I must stay at your house today" (5).
"The Lord blessed the whole house of Obed-Edom and every one of those with him" (11).	"Today salvation has come to this house" (9).

2 Kgdms 6:1–10, imitated by Luke 19:11–27

The ark of the covenant has been kept at the home of Amminadab in Kiriath-Jearim, located some ten miles from Jerusalem (see 1 Kgdms 7:1), before it was carted to a place close to Jerusalem (2 Kgdms 6:3–10).	"He was near Jerusalem, and . . . they supposed that the kingdom of God was to appear immediately" (19:11).
"David . . . went . . . to bring up from there the Ark of God on which (was) the name of the Lord Almighty" (2).	"A nobleman went to a distant country to get royal power for himself and then return" (12).
"Uzzah and his brothers" led the wagon with the ark (3–4).	"He summoned ten of his slaves . . . and said to them, 'Do business with these'" (13).
"David was terrified of the Lord," who had become wrathful (9).	"I was afraid of you, because you are a harsh man" (21).
"God struck him down right there" (7).	"Bring them here and slaughter them in my presence" (27).

2 Kgdms 6:1–23, imitated by Luke 19:28–44; 13:34–35

The table below notes thematic parallels between 2 Kingdoms 6:1–23 and two Lukan passages. First, the evangelist registers parallels to the ark's royal arrival in Jerusalem (6:1–19) by a Gospel text describing Jesus' royal arrival to the same city (19:11–38). Second, Luke acknowledges parallels to Michal's disgust and confrontation with David (2 Kgdms 6:16, 20–23) by Jesus' lament in Luke 19:39–44, combined with Jesus' dismissal of Herod's threat (13:34–35, *in its bookend role*).[12]

12. Luke also placed 13:34–35 in the center of the journey narrative to

"He loaded the Ark of the Lord onto a new wagon" (6:3).	"You will find tied there a colt that has never been ridden" (19:30).
"David and the sons of Israel were dancing before the Lord" with songs and various instruments (5). "David and all the house of Israel brought up the Ark of the Lord with shouting and with the sound of the trumpet" (15).	"The whole multitude of the disciples began to praise God joyfully with a loud voice" (37).
Of twenty-four occurrences of David's name in these verses, twice the narrator calls him "King David" (12, 16).	"'Blessed is the king who comes in the name of the Lord!'" (38).
Michal "despised him in her heart" (16) and rebuked David (20).	"Teacher, order your disciples to stop" (39).
David informs Michal that "I will dance" (21), "I will play music and dance" (21), "I will uncover myself again" (22).	"I tell you, if these were silent, the stones would shout out" (40).
David knows that he will be "useless" in Michal's eyes (22).	"Now they are hidden from your eyes" (42). "You did not recognize the time of your visitation from God" (44).
"David returned to bless" (20).	"Blessed is the king who comes in the name of the Lord!" (38).
"The Lord . . . chose me over your father and over his entire house to appoint me as the leader over his people" (21).	"See, your house is left to you" (13:35).
"For Michal daughter of Saul, there was no child even until the day of her death" (23).	"How often have I desired to gather your children together as a hen gathers her brood under her wings, and you were not willing!" (34).

As we have seen, Luke selects episodes from the Jesus tradition, organizes them, and edits them into narrative reflections (Luke 9:51—19:44) of David's odyssey (1 Kgdms 19:11—2 Kgdms 6:23). The contexts both of model and reflection show other similarities. Not only do the *contexts before* David's odyssey and before Jesus'

---

parallel David's lament over Saul and Jonathan in 2 Kgdms 1. See page 13 above.

journey recount mountaintop epiphanies of God, but analogously, the *contexts after* both odyssey and journey narrate that King David and King Jesus each enter the temple of God. In 2 Kingdoms 7, David enters the temple to express his amazement and gratitude in prayer for God's covenant promise to establish David's throne forever. In Luke 19, following his lament over Jerusalem, Jesus enters the temple and reasserts its use as a house of prayer (45–46). Thereafter, Jesus daily enters the temple to teach (19:47—21:38). Texts before and after Jesus' journey, as well as the journey's many episodes, richly reflect David's odyssey. Luke organizes and edits a complex reflection of David's odyssey in Jesus' journey.

The Gospel writer, however, organizes an even more complex paralleling project: he also imitates stories of Moses and the Judges *using the same journey chapters* of his Gospel. We next follow Luke's project of paralleling Moses from the book of Numbers, using the first half of the same gospel episodes by which we see reflections of David's odyssey.

> I had no idea.
>
> Num 22:34 (*MSG*)

> You don't have to be a genius to understand these things.
>
> Luke 12:57 (*MSG*)

3

Luke's Imitation of Moses as Deliverer

David P. Moessner produced a famous and rigorous study, *Lord of the Banquet*, describing a Deuteronomy-based Moses/Exodus motif in Luke's journey narrative (or Central Section), beginning in Luke 9:1–50, continuing in the Central Section, and broadly in all of Luke and Acts.[1] Moessner concludes that

> What sets the Central Section apart from its counterparts is the development of a consistent typology based on the Moses of Deuteronomy to form a coherent drama of a New Exodus for the Prophet Jesus who is the prophet like Moses.[2]

Our study of the Central Section, or journey narrative as we call it, also detects that the narrative exhibits a sustained connection to the story of Moses as he led Israel in the Exodus.[3] While theology from the book of Deuteronomy certainly pervades Luke's theological vision, *the literary tie* to Moses and the Exodus connects

---

1. Moessner, *Lord of the Banquet*.
2. Moessner, *Lord of the Banquet*, 260.
3. We detect a sustained connection to the story of Moses even though the name "Moses" appears only in two places (Luke 16:29, 31) in the journey narrative, and his name does not appear at all in the first half of the journey narrative (Luke 9:51—13:33).

Luke's Imitation of Moses as Deliverer

Luke 9:51—13:33 with *the book of Numbers*, beginning at Numbers 10:11 and continuing to the end of that book.[4] The book of Numbers also has resources that Luke needs for his project, resources that Deuteronomy lacks: narrative length and a neutral narrator.

In Deuteronomy, Moses provides only three chapters of summary for Israel's journey from Horeb to Pisgah (chs. 1–3), while Numbers offers many chapters of narrative resources for Luke's lengthy paralleling activity. Further, in Deuteronomy 1–3 Moses' words narrate his story as a first-person account ("I, we") while Numbers exhibits the neutral third-person perspective ("he, they"), the same voice as in most Gospel episodes. Therefore, the language of Numbers proves more useful for Luke than the language of Deuteronomy in arranging Gospel imitations of Israel's journey. The same narrative voice in both model and parallel allows many parallels to be clear-cut and distinct.

Before turning to the whole catalog of parallels, let us especially notice a few of the most distinct model-to-echo similarities and the densest clusters of model-to-echo similarities.

DISTINCT THEMATIC IMITATIONS

Our exploration discovers many clear-cut parallels between details of Moses' leadership over Israel (from Sinai to the Jordan) in the book of Numbers and the Lukan journey. Even though the Numbers model extends through a full twenty-four chapters of that book, sequential parallels between Numbers and the much shorter Luke 9:51—13:33 can readily be identified.[5]

---

4. Moessner seems not to consider this possibility, as evidenced in the index to *Lord of the Banquet*. Nearly four pages list his references to the book of Deuteronomy (340–43), while the author refers to Numbers (which contains the same story) only seven times (340).

5. Literary connections between the Lukan journey and the book of Numbers are less transparent than are the ties between David's odyssey (see ch. 2) and the Lukan journey, but nonetheless definite. One reason for this is that the first half of Luke's journey narrative (just over four chapters of Luke) parallels some twenty-four chapters in Numbers. Second, Luke makes a compositional choice to deselect legal statutes in Numbers as models for imitation. For four extended groups of statutes Luke provides no parallels (Num 18:1—19:22;

33

Kings, Deliverers, and Prophets in Luke's Journey Narrative

Certain textual parallels catch our attention by *brief but sharp model-to-echo similarity*, as in these selected examples:

Numbers	Luke
The Lord responds, "Gather together to me seventy men" (11:16). Moses gathers seventy men to help lead the people. The Lord endows the seventy with Moses' spirit, but two other qualified leaders remain in camp. They also receive the endowment, making a total of seventy-two leaders to help Moses (16–26).	"Lord appointed seventy others" (in some manuscripts, "seventy-two") in teams of two for preparing towns for Jesus' arrival (10:1).
Caleb silences the people and declares that we "will overpower them" (13:31). But some of the spies insist, "We are not able to go up against the people, because they are very much stronger than we are" (32).	"Whoever listens to you listens to me, and whoever rejects you rejects me, and whoever rejects me rejects the one who sent me" (10:16).
"All those dwelling on this land have heard that you yourself are the Lord, among this people, who appears to them eyes to eyes" (14:14).	"Blessed are the eyes that see what you see! For I tell you that many prophets and kings desired to see what you see, but did not see it, and to hear what you hear, but did not hear it" (10:23–24).
"Whenever you completely fail" (15:22) or "involuntarily" sin (24–27), "it will be forgiven" (26) through atonement by sacrifice (25–26).	"Forgive us our sins" (11:4).
Separate from "these stubborn people" (16:26): Korah, Dathan, Abiram, and their supporters.	This is "an evil generation" that will face judgment (11:29).

26:1—27:11; 28:1—30:17; 33:50—36:13). After each group of statutes, when narrative resumes, Luke immediately resumes imitating features in Numbers.

Luke's Imitation of Moses as Deliverer

Israel ganged up against Moses and Aaron (16:42).	Scribes and Pharisees "began to be very hostile toward him and to cross-examine him about many things, lying in wait for him, to catch him in something he might say" (11:53–54).
God came to Balaam by night (22:10, 20).	"The Son of Man is coming at an unexpected hour" (12:40).

In other textual places we see sequential parallels between *dense groups of features* in Numbers and dense groups of Lukan features. Luke 9:51–62 densely imitates Numbers 10:11—11:3. Luke 12:8–12 follows Numbers 20:1–13 closely. Finally, Luke 13:22–28 tightly imitates Numbers 32:1–42.

Num 10:11—11:3, densely imitated by Luke 9:51-62

The sons of Israel "set out at the direction of the Lord by the hand of Moses" (10:13).	Jesus "set his face to go to Jerusalem" (9:51).
"The ark of the covenant of the Lord went on ahead of them . . . seeking out for them a resting place" (10:34).	"He sent messengers ahead of him." ". . . to make ready for him" (52).
The Lord "was provoked with anger. And a fire was kindled among them from the Lord, and it devoured a certain portion of the encampment" (11:1).	"Do you want us to command fire to come down from heaven and consume them?" (54).
"Come with us" (10:29).	"Follow me" (59).
"We are setting out for the (unknown) place concerning which the Lord said, 'This I will give to you'" (10:29).	"Wherever you go . . ." (57).
"I will not go along, but I will go into my own land and to my own people" (10:30).	"I will follow you, Lord, but let me first say farewell to those at my home" (61).

Num 20:1–13, densely imitated by Luke 12:8–12

When Moses strikes the rock instead of speaking to it as the Lord had instructed him to do (Num 20:11), Moses does not "sanctify" the Lord "before the sons of Israel" (12).	"Everyone who acknowledges me before others, the Son of Man will also acknowledge before the angels of God; but whoever denies me before others will be denied before the angels of God" (Luke 12:8–9).
The congregation (*synagogē*) "gathered themselves against Moses and Aaron. And the people railed against Moses" (2–3).	"When they bring you before the synagogues, the rulers, and the authorities . . ." (Luke 12:11).
Moses and Aaron went "from the face of the congregation to the entrance of the tent of testimony, and they fell on their faces . . ." (6).	". . . do not worry about how you are to defend yourself or what you are to say; . . ." (12:11).
". . . and then the glory of the Lord appeared to them" (6). And the Lord instructed them what to do (7).	". . . for the Holy Spirit will teach you in that very hour what you ought to say" (12:12).

Num 32:1–42, densely imitated by Luke 13:22–28

Listed Transjordan towns that the Lord delivered to Israel are Ataroth, Dibon, Jazer, Nimrah, Heshbon, Elealeh, Sebam, Nebo, and Beon (Num 32:3).	Jesus "went through one town and village after another" (Luke 13:22).
"Do not make us cross over the Jordan" (5).	"Strive to enter through the narrow door" (24).
"These people . . . did not follow closely after me" (11).	The master of the house says, "Go away from me, all you evildoers!" (27).
"These people who came up out of Egypt . . ." will not "see the land that he promised" to the patriarchs (11).	"Many . . . will try to enter and will not be able" (24).

Luke's Imitation of Moses as Deliverer

Reubenites and Gadites "are arming" themselves "as an advanced guard for the (rest of) the sons of Israel, until" they "bring them to their own territory" (17). "We will not return back to our houses until all the sons of Israel have been apportioned" (18).	"Some are last who will be first, and some are first who will be last" (30).

The compact Lukan passages above exhibit dense parallels to episodes in Numbers. Such densely clustered echoes in Luke and many other parallels alert readers of Luke's journey narrative to look more broadly in Numbers for other parallels. With this preparation of our textual vision, we provide next a catalog of imitations between the Greek OT model and Luke's narrative (including all the examples given above but put in their respective places in the sequences).

LUKE'S IMITATIONS OF NUMBERS 10:11—36:13 IN LUKE 9:51—13:33

Luke 13:31-33 serves *both* as an essential middle block of journey text *and* as a journey bookend text.[6] *As a bookend text*, Luke 13:31-33 connects to the beginning of Jesus' journey, and may be read there as the very beginning of the beginning of the journey. Thus, Luke's echoes of Moses and Israel in Numbers begin at Luke 13:31-33 and then continue in 9:51-56.

Num 10:11-36, traced by Luke 13:31-33

Israel "set out" (8x) from Sinai in the Lord's prescribed order and on the Lord's chosen day (Num 10:11–35).	Jesus declares his deliberate intention to "be on my way," in his own time and for his own purpose (Luke 13:32–33).
"Let your enemies be scattered, let all those who hate you flee!" (10:35).	"Go tell that fox" (32) that Herod's supposed prey does not flee or cease his ministry.

---

6. See Appendix 1 for further explanation.

"They set out from the mountain of the Lord on a journey of three days, and the ark of the covenant of the Lord went on ahead of them on a journey of three days" (33).	Jesus has ministry to do, unhindered, "today and tomorrow, and on the third day he will finish his work" (32). "Yet, today, and tomorrow, and the next day I must be on my way" (33).
Each tribe of Israel has its work assignment related to the logistics of the journey (17, 21, 28).	"On the third day I finish my work" (32).

Num 10:11—11:3, imitated by Luke 9:51-62

The sons of Israel "set out at the direction of the Lord by the hand of Moses" (Num 10:13).	Jesus "set his face to go to Jerusalem" (Luke 9:51).
"The ark of the covenant of the Lord went on ahead of them . . . seeking out for them a resting place" (34).	"He sent messengers ahead of him. . . . to make ready for him" (52).
The Lord "was provoked with anger. And a fire was kindled among them from the Lord, and it devoured a certain portion of the encampment" (11:1).	"Do you want us to command fire to come down from heaven and consume them?" (54).
"Come with us" (10:29).	"Follow me" (59).
"We are setting out for the (unknown) place concerning which the Lord said, 'This I will give to you'" (29).	"Wherever you go . . ." (57).
"I will not go along, but I will go into my own land and to my own people" (30).	"I will follow you, Lord, but let me first say farewell to those at my home" (61).

Num 11:1—13:30, paralleled by Luke 10:1-16

In Numbers 13 of the LXX, verse numbers differ by one from Numbers 13 in the Hebrew Bible. Subtracting one from the Numbers 13 (LXX) verse numbers obtains Numbers 13 (NRSV) verse numbers.

Luke's Imitation of Moses as Deliverer

Moses complains, "I myself alone am not able to carry this people, because this matter is too heavy for me" (Num 11:14).	"The harvest is plentiful, but the laborers are few; therefore ask the Lord of the harvest to send out laborers into his harvest" (Luke 10:2).
The Lord responds, "Gather together to me seventy men" (16). So Moses gathers seventy men to help lead the people. The Lord endows the seventy gathered men with Moses' spirit, but two other qualified leaders remain in camp. They also receive the endowment, making a total of seventy-two leaders to help Moses (16–26).	"Lord appointed seventy others" (seventy-two?) in teams of two for preparing towns for Jesus' arrival (10:1).
Inside the camp, Joshua becomes frantic over the apparently unauthorized prophesying of two men. Moses, however, is glad for their additional help (27–30).	The disciples should look for persons of peace (5–6).
The spirit of Moses rests on the seventy-two (26, 29).	Peace will "rest on" any sons of peace who are present (6).
For those in Israel who craved meat, the Lord "swept along quails" on a wind that "blew them on the encampment." But the Lord struck down those who craved (31–34).	Eat and drink "whatever they provide" (7). "Eat what is set before you" (8).
"The Lord descended in a pillar of cloud and stood at the entrance to the tent of testimony" (12:5).	"The kingdom of God has come near to you" (9, 11).
"O God, I beseech you to heal" Miriam (13)!	"Cure the sick" in houses of those who host you (9).
"The people dwelling on it are strong, and the cities are fortified with walls and exceedingly large" (13:29).	"Woe" to cities: Chorazin, Bethsaida, Tyre, Sidon, Capernaum (13–15).
Caleb silences the people and declares that we "will overpower them" (31). But some of the spies insist, "We are not able to go up against the people, because they are very much stronger than we are" (32).	"Whoever listens to you listens to me, and whoever rejects you rejects me, and whoever rejects me rejects the one who sent me" (16).

Num 13:26—14:25, contrasted by Luke 10:17-24

The spies "came to Moses and Aaron . . . and they related to them a verbal report and to the whole assembly, and they showed the fruit of the land" (Num 13:27).	"The seventy returned (to Jesus) with joy, saying, 'Lord, in your name even the demons submit to us!'" (Luke 10:17).
"We have seen the offspring of Anak there" (29). "There we have seen the giants" (34).	Jesus saw the kingdom's adversary, Satan (18).
"They are very much stronger than we are" (32). "We were, compared to them, like locusts" (34).	"See, I have given you authority to tread on snakes and scorpions, and over all the power of the enemy; and nothing will hurt you" (19).
"The entire community lifted up and sounded with a voice, and the people wept throughout that night" (14:1). They want to return to Egypt.	"Do not rejoice in this, that the spirits submit to you, but rejoice that your names are written in heaven" (20).
"As I myself live, and as my name also lives, the glory of the Lord will fill all the earth" (21).	"Father, Lord of heaven and earth . . ." (21).
"You were merciful to (this people) since they came from Egypt until right now" (19).	"Such was your gracious will" (21).
Those who saw the signs in Egypt and yet tested and provoked the Lord "will not see the land that I swore to their fathers" (23). Instead, to their children "I will give the land" (24).	"You have hidden these things from the wise and intelligent and have revealed them to infants" (21).
"All those dwelling on this land have heard that you yourself are the Lord, among this people, who appears to them eyes to eyes" (14).	"Blessed are the eyes that see what you see! For I tell you that many prophets and kings desired to see what you see, but did not see it, and to hear what you hear, but did not hear it" (23-24).

Num 14:20—15:10, reflected by Luke 10:25-37

The men who "put me to the test . . ." (Num 14:22).	"A lawyer stood up to test Jesus" (Luke 10:25).

Luke's Imitation of Moses as Deliverer

"... and have not obeyed my voice" (14:22).	"Teacher, he said, ..." (10:25).
"My servant Caleb ... will inherit it" (24).	"... what must I do to inherit eternal life?" (10:25).
My servant Caleb had "a different spirit in him, and he followed me closely" (24).	"You shall love the Lord your God with all your heart, and with all your soul, and with all your strength, and with all your mind; and your neighbor as yourself" (27).
Israel, being "persistent and forceful, they went up to the high regions of the hill country" (44). Those "living in that mountainous area came down and put them to flight" (45).	"A man was going down (the bandit-infested road) from Jerusalem to Jericho" (30).
"You will fall" (42) before the Amalekites and Canaanites. "You will fall by the sword" (43). The ambushers "put them to flight and cut them down" (45).	He "fell into the hands of robbers, who stripped him, beat him ... leaving him half dead" (30).
Various homecoming sacrifices upon entering the land include oil and wine (15:4–10).	"He ... bandaged his wounds, having poured oil and wine on them" (34).
One variety of sacrifice could be "to honor (fulfill) a vow" (3).	The Samaritan promised to cover any further expenses required for the recovery of the Israelite man: "I will repay you whatever more you spend" (35).

Num 15:11–31, imitated by Luke 10:38–42

If "an alien" takes up residence among you ... (Num 15:14, 15 [2x], 16, 29).	Martha "welcomed (Jesus) into her home" (Luke 10:38).
One law (*heis*) for both Israel and guest (15, 16, 29). One sacrificial animal (*heis*, 12, 24 [2x]). One person (*mia*, 27), one goat (*mia*, 27).	"There is need of only one (*henos*) thing" (42).

Num 15:22–41, suggested by Luke 11:1–13

"Fringes" on "flaps of their garments" may be related to prayer shawls (Num 15:38).	"Lord, teach us to pray" (Luke 11:1). "When you pray, say" (2).
"A blue thread" is a reference to kingly authority and to God's rule (38).	"'. . . your kingdom come'" (2).
"Whenever you completely fail" (22) or "involuntarily" sin (24–27), "it will be forgiven" (26) through atonement by sacrifice (25–26).	"'Forgive us our sins . . .'" (4).
"They found a man gathering wood on the Sabbath day" (32).	A friend on a journey arrives at midnight. The host seeks bread from his neighbor at midnight (5).
"They put him under guard" (34).	"The door has already been locked, and my children are with me in bed; I cannot get up and give you anything" (7).
"They had not decided what they should do concerning him" (34).	The neighbor changes his mind (8).
You will "be holy to your God" (40).	"Hallowed (holy) be your name" (2). "The heavenly Father" will "give the Holy Spirit to those who ask him!" (13).

Num 16:1–22, echoed by Luke 11:14–28

Levites led by Korah, Dathan, and Abiram mount a leadership challenge to Moses and Aaron. The challengers claim that "all are holy" (Num 16:3) and all want to be priests.	Some who see an exorcism by Jesus claim that he does it by demonic power. Some others do not accept the sign-value of the exorcism, and they want a more believable sign (Luke 11:15–16).
The challengers enjoy the support of 250 primary Israelite leaders (2).	"Every kingdom divided against itself . . ." (17).
"They stood together against Moses and Aaron" (3).	"House falls on house" (17).
Korah and all his group have "gathered together against God" (11).	"Whoever is not with me is against me, and whoever does not gather with me scatters" (23).

Luke's Imitation of Moses as Deliverer

The challengers claim, "You brought us up into a land flowing with milk and honey to slay us in the wilderness" (13).	A spirit passes through waterless places seeking rest, and finding none it says, "I will return to my house from which I came" (24).
"Korah drew up against them his entire assembly beside the entrance of the tent of testimony" (19).	"It goes and brings seven other spirits" to enter and dwell in the house (26).
God already knows the ones who are to be priests, "and he [leads] them to himself" (5).	Blessed "are those who hear the word of God and obey it" (28).

Num 16:23-35, imitated by Luke 11:29-32

Separate from "these stubborn people" (Num 16:26): Korah, Dathan, Abiram, and their supporters.	This is "an evil generation" that will face judgment (Luke 11:29).
"If by a sign the Lord shows it clearly . . ." (30).	This generation "asks for a sign" (29).
They will go down "alive into Hades (30)." "The earth opened and swallowed them" (32). Israelites flee, crying, "What if the earth devours us?" (34).	"Judgment" (31, 32); "condemn" (31, 32). "The sign of Jonah"* will be given to this generation (29).
	*See expressions comparable to Num 16:30-34 in Jonah 2:6 LXX: "the abyss surrounds me;" "my head withdraws into the cleft of the hill."

Num 16:36-40, figured by Luke 11:33-36

Fire is put on a brass censer to burn incense (Num 16:36-40).	A lamp is put on a lampstand to give light (Luke 11:33).
Only offspring of Aaron may legitimately place incense before the Lord (40).	"If your eye is healthy . . ." (34).
"No unqualified person" may "place incense before the Lord" (40).	"If it (your eye) is not healthy . . ." (34).

Num 16:41–50 accords with Luke 11:37–54

Moses and Aaron "entered by the front of the tent of testimony" (Num 16:43).	Jesus "went in and took his place at the table" (Luke 11:37).
"I will utterly destroy them immediately" (45).	"Woe to you . . ." (42, 43, 44).
"You yourselves have killed the people of the Lord" (41).	"You build the tombs of the prophets whom your ancestors killed" (47).
Fourteen thousand seven hundred additional people died until Aaron took fire from the altar to make atonement for the people and then return to the tent of testimony. (47–50)	Zechariah "perished between the altar and the sanctuary" (51).
Israel ganged up against Moses and Aaron (42).	Scribes and Pharisees "began to be very hostile toward him and to cross-examine him about many things, lying in wait for him, to catch him in something he might say" (53–54).

Num 17:1–13, echoed by Luke 12:1–7

God acts to quell Israel's continual "murmuring" against Moses and Aaron (Num 17:5).	"Whatever you have said in the dark will be heard in the light, and what you have whispered behind closed doors will be proclaimed from the housetops" (Luke 12:3).
"We are perishing; we are utterly destroyed; we are consumed" (12).	"Do not fear those who kill the body" (4). "Fear him who, after he has killed, has authority to cast into hell!" (5).

Luke does not organize parallels to Numbers 18:1—19:22 because he excludes legal statutes as sources for his parallels. Luke echoes only narrative portions of Numbers.

Luke's Imitation of Moses as Deliverer

Num 20:1-13, imitated by Luke 12:8-12

Moses strikes the rock instead of speaking to it as the Lord had instructed him to do. Moses does not "sanctify" the Lord "before the sons of Israel" (Num 20:12).	"Everyone who acknowledges me before others, the Son of Man also will acknowledge before the angels of God; but whoever denies me before others will be denied before the angels of God" (Luke 12:8-9).
The "congregation" (*synagogē*) "gathered themselves against Moses and Aaron" (2). "And the people railed against Moses" (3).	"When they bring you before the synagogues, the rulers, and the authorities . . ." (11).
Moses and Aaron went "from the face of the congregation to the entrance of the tent of testimony, and they fell on their faces . . ." (6).	". . . do not worry about how you are to defend yourself or what you are to say; . . ." (11).
". . . and then the glory of the Lord appeared to them" (7). Then the Lord instructed them what to do (8).	". . . for the Holy Spirit will teach you in that very hour what you ought to say" (12).

Num 20:14—21:1-35, matched by Luke 12:13-32

Moses requests of the king of Edom: "Your brother Israel says" (Num 20:14), let us pass through. (17)	Someone in the crowd asked Jesus to "Tell my brother" to divide an inheritance. (Luke 12:13)
Moses promises that Israel will not loot or pillage while Israel passes through Edom's fields and vineyards (17).	"The land of a rich man produced abundantly" (16).
"You provoked me" is the reason for Aaron's imminent death (24).	"So it is with those who . . . are not rich toward God" (21).
"Aaron died at the top of the mountain" (28).	"This very night your life is being demanded of you" (20).
The Lord instructs Moses to strip Aaron of his priestly cloak and put it instead on Eleazar (26-28).	"The body" is "more than clothing" (23). If God arrays the lilies with such beauty, "how much more will he clothe you!" (28).

45

"For what purpose is this, that you have led us out of Egypt to slay us in the wilderness? Because there is no food or water, and our soul (*psychē*) is weary with this meager food" (21:5).	"Do not worry about your life (*psychē*), what you will eat" (22). "Life (*psychē*) is more than food" (23). "Do not keep striving for what you are to eat and what you are to drink, and do not keep worrying" (29).
"Kings of nations" dug the well (18).	The nations of the world "strive after all these things" (30).
"Do not fear" Og, king of Bashan (34).	"Do not be afraid, little flock, ..." (32).
"... for I have given him and all his people and all his land into your hands" (34). God struck him and gave his land to Israel (35).	"... for it is your Father's good pleasure to give you the kingdom" (32).

Num 22:1—24:25, imaged by Luke 12:33-59

"The elders of Moab" went to Balaam with payment for divination "in their hands" (Num 22:7). "Even if Balak gives me his house filled with silver and gold, I am not able" (18).	"Make purses for yourselves that do not wear out" (Luke 12:33).
When the elders of Moab came, Balaam said, "Remain here during the night" (8, 19).	Slaves await their master's return home at some unknown hour of the night (35–40).
God came to Balaam by night (9, 20).	"The Son of Man is coming at an unexpected hour" (40).
Balaam "struck the donkey" (23), then Balaam "continued to further whip it" (25), and "struck the donkey with a rod" (27).	A slave "begins to beat" other slaves (45). Disobedient slaves receive "a severe beating" (47), and others "a light beating" (48).
A messenger of the Lord had "a drawn sword in his hand" (23, 31). The messenger "would have slain" Balaam (33).	The master will make a surprise return and "cut (the presumptuous slave) in pieces, and put him with the unfaithful" (45–46).
Balak hopes to buy Balaam's service: "I will honor you honorably, and whatever you may say I will do for you. And so, come! Put a curse for me on this people" (17).	"From everyone to whom much has been given, much will be required, and from the one to whom much has been entrusted, even more will be demanded" (48).

LUKE'S IMITATION OF MOSES AS DELIVERER

Balaam's final oracle lists five nations that will face eventual disruption: Moab, Edom, Amalek, the Kenites, and Og (24:17–24).

"From now on five in one house will be divided, three against two and two against three" (52).

King Balak sees that "this multitude will lick up everything that is around us as an ox licks up the green herbs of the field" (22:4). Yet, Balak seeks a curse to stop them (4–20).

When you see (a cloud, south wind) you say (a shower, scorching heat) is coming (54–55). "Why do you not know how to interpret the present time?" (56).

Balaam appeals to the angel of God: "I did not know that you yourself were opposing me in the road to confront me, and now, if it does not seem good to you, I will turn back" (34).

"Why do you not judge for yourselves what is right?" (57). "When you go with your accuser . . . on the way make an effort to settle the case" (58).

Num 25:1–18 pairs with Luke 13:1–5

"Slay, each one, anyone of his household who is now consecrated to Baal-peor" (Num 25:5).

Pilate mingled blood of Galileans with their sacrifices (Luke 13:1).

"Twenty-four thousand" Israelite leaders who did obeisance to Moabite gods die in a plague (9).

"All other" sinners (2, 4).

An Israelite man and a Moabite woman have sex in the tent of witness (6–8).

Are these "worse sinners" than the others (2, 4)?

"Twenty-four thousand" die in a plague of judgment, and the man and woman die, skewered together to the ground by Phinehas's spear (8–9).

"Unless you repent, you will all perish just as they did" (5).

Luke excludes the legal statutes of Numbers 26:1—27:11 from his imitation, and skips to the following:

Num 27:12–23 links to Luke 13:6–17

Moses has been God's chosen leader for Israel.

"A man had a fig tree planted in his vineyard" (Luke 13:6).

47

"You transgressed (God's) word in the desert wilderness of Zin, when the congregation refused to sanctify me. You did not sanctify me with regard to the water in their presence" (Num 27:14).	The man finds no fruit on his fig tree (6).
In consequence, "You will be added to your people, even you yourself, just as Aaron, your brother, was" (13).	"Cut it down!" (7).
Moses urges, "Let the Lord . . . diligently attend to a (replacement leadership) person over this congregation" (16).	The vinedresser urges that fertilizer be applied first, before giving up on the tree (8).
Moses continues in leadership for a few months (Num 31:2).	"Let (the tree) alone for one more year" (8).
Joshua, son of Nun, "a man who has the spirit in himself" (18).	A woman shows up who has a "spirit that had crippled her" (11).
"Place your hands on him" (18). "You will place your authority on him" (20). "He placed his hands on him" (23).	"When he laid his hands on her . . ." (13).
"He will stand before Eleazar, the priest" (21). Moses "stood him before Eleazar, the priest, and before the entire congregation" (22).	". . . immediately she stood up straight . . ." (13).
"The entire congregation (*synagogē*)" (19, 21, 22).	The "leader of the synagogue" was "indignant" (14).

Again, Luke includes only narrative as the model for his imitation, leaving out Numbers 28:1—30:17.

Num 31:1–54, traced by Luke 13:18–21

Before the battle with Midian, "twelve thousands, armed for battle" set out from the camp (Num 31:5).	The kingdom of God is "like a mustard seed" (Luke 13:19).
The abundance of the plunder was: 675,000 sheep, 72,000 oxen, 61,000 donkeys, 32,000 human souls (32–35).	The seed "grew and became a tree . . ." (19).

Luke's Imitation of Moses as Deliverer

"One out of fifty" (30, 47) captured humans and livestock are a levy to the Lord for the Levites.	". . . and the birds of the air made nests in its branches" (19).
Eleazar took a thank offering (52) on behalf of the warriors (16,750 shekels of gold) into the tent of witness as a memorial before the Lord. (54)	The kingdom of God is like leaven hidden in flour (20–21).

Num 32:1–42, imitated by Luke 13:22–28

Listed Transjordan towns that the Lord delivered to Israel: Ataroth, Dibon, Jazer, Nimrah, Heshbon, Elealeh, Sebam, Nebo, and Beon (Num 32:3).	Jesus "went through one town and village after another" (Luke 13:22).
"Do not make us cross over the Jordan" (5).	"Strive to enter through the narrow door" (24).
"These people . . . did not follow closely after me" (11).	The master of the house says, "Go away from me, all you evildoers!" (27).
"These people who came up out of Egypt . . ." shall not "see the land that he promised" to the patriarchs (11).	"Many . . . will try to enter and will not be able" (24).
Reubenites and Gadites "are arming ourselves for battle as an advanced guard for the (rest of) Israel, until we bring them into their own territory" (17). "We will not turn back to our houses until all the sons of Israel have been apportioned" (18).	"Some are last who will be first, and some are first who will be last" (30).

Num 33:1–49, reflected by Luke 13:31–33

"The sons of Israel went forth" from the land of Egypt (33:3). "And the Egyptians were burying the dead among them" (Num 33:4).	"Get away from here, for Herod wants to kill you" (Luke 13:31).
"The sons of Israel went forth with an upraised hand in defiance before all the Egyptians" (3).	Jesus goes away on his own schedule and for his own purposes: "I must be on my way" (33).

Luke excludes Numbers 33:50—36:13 due to its genre as statutes, commandments, and judgments (see 36:13). The same has been true of Numbers 18:1—19:22, 26:1—27:11, and 28:1—30:17. Luke does not match these legal texts with gospel texts; instead, he develops parallels only for narrative portions of Numbers.

Episodes about Jesus in Luke 9:51—13:33, up to the journey's middle, imitate episodes of Moses' leadership in Numbers from Num 10:11 to the book's end, except for legal portions. In Luke, however, Jesus' journey continues for a few more chapters. The evangelist does not terminate his parallels of God's deliverer when he exhausts the book of Numbers; rather, Luke picks up the thread of deliverer from another OT narrative.

The canonical order of OT books and the overall plot of Israel's story offer us reasonable places to search for imitable continuations. For one, Deuteronomy comes next in the ancient canon, but Lukan text beginning at 13:34 *does not* echo any initial chapters of Deuteronomy. Second, the book of Joshua furthers the story of Israel crossing the Jordan and invading the promised land. The LXX title for this OT book, "*Iēsous*" (Joshua), matches the angel-given name of Jesus in Luke: *Iēsous* (Luke 1:32). But for all that the book of Joshua may seem to suggest as an imitable model for Luke, his text beginning from Luke 13:34 *does not* echo the initial chapters of Joshua.

Luke 13:33-35, beginning the second half of Jesus' journey, prominently features the city of Jerusalem over which Jesus laments. While the beginnings of Deuteronomy and Joshua offer no lexical or thematic connections to "Jerusalem," the beginning of Judges (LXX) does. And significantly so, for three reasons. First, "Jerusalem (*Ierousalēm*)" occurs four times in the first twenty-two verses of Judges (1:7, 8, 21, 22). This city name occurs in Judges *anachronistically* (instead of the pre-Davidic ancient city name *Jebus* that labels its occupants as Jebusites).[7] Second, the text of Luke 13:33-34 has three iterations of *Ierousalēm* side by side, an extremely unusual grouping of one name.[8] The literary curiosity of

---

7. Anachronistic use of "Jerusalem" points to a composition date for these verses during or after the kingship of David. See Judg 1:21 for tight juxtaposing of the terms "Jebusite" and "Jerusalem."

8. "It is impossible for a prophet to be killed outside Jerusalem. Jerusalem,

Luke's Imitation of Moses as Deliverer

a tripled city name in Luke 13 echoes the literary curiosity of the same city name occurring anachronistically four times in Judges 1. Third, Luke has been imitating an OT historical narrative that ends with the appointment of Joshua (*Iēsous*) to lead Israel into Canaan. Then he shifts to another OT historical narrative that begins "after the death of Joshua (*Iēsous*)" (Judg 1:1). That Luke skips over Joshua's career as leader in war affirms that Jesus should not be viewed as conqueror of nations. Instead, Jesus should be seen as God's deliverer (Savior) from bondage, just as God delivered Israel by the hand of Moses and delivered Israel by the hand of his judges.[9] Moses is a God-empowered deliverer and so also are the judges of Israel as described in the book of Judges. Luke portrays Jesus not as a new Moses *per se*, but as God's new deliverer.[10]

Jerusalem, the city that kills..." (Luke 13:33-34). NT Greek manuscripts have no spaces or punctuation between words. Three iterations of the indeclinable city name stand side by side.

9. The noun *sōtēr* (deliverer, savior) and the verb *sōzein* (deliver, save) describe God and God's purposes for Israel by means of Moses (Exod 3:8-10) and by means of Judges (*sōtēr*: Judg 3:9, 15; *sōzein*: 2:16, 18; 3:9, 31; 6:14, 15, 31, 36, 37; 7:2, 7; 8:22; 10:1; 13:5).

10. In 9:51—19:44, Luke does not echo Moses' leadership as receiver of God's law on Mt. Horeb (Exod 19—Num 9), even though in Luke, Moses talks with Jesus on the Mount of Transfiguration (Luke 9:28-36) and in the journey narrative Jesus teaches about the law (10:26-28; 16:16; 18:20-22, 31). Luke does not echo themes from Moses' sermons in Deuteronomy (1–34), presumably because that book primarily reviews and clarifies God's law rather than narrates Israel's story. Luke does not, in Luke 9–19, parallel Jesus to Moses per se, but only Moses as one of God's OT savior-redeemers in circumstances when Levantine powers resist God's people and when God's savior-redeemers exhibit crippling character flaws (including that of Moses, Num 20:9-12). One may find allusions to Moses' lawgiving in the journey narrative, but they remain isolated echoes. The journey narrative does not reflect Joshua's leadership (Josh 1–24), probably because in that book Israel no longer journeys, and because Joshua is not a deliverer but a conqueror. Luke does not characterize Jesus as a conqueror of nations; on the contrary, Jesus is a suffering, dying Savior. Luke does, however, portray Jesus as a conqueror of Satan (4:34; 8:28; 10:17-19; 11:20-23).

> Stay here with me. Be my father and priest.
>
> JUDG 17:10 (*MSG*)

> Zacchaeus, hurry down.
> Today is my day to be a guest in your home.
>
> LUKE 19:6 (*MSG*)

4
Luke's Parallels of Judges as Deliverers

DAVID I. BLOCK, IN his commentary, *Judges/Ruth*, assesses ways that New Testament writers interpret the book of Judges:

> References to the book of Judges are rare in the New Testament. Usually the allusions are to persons or events analogous to New Testament counterparts.[1]

Three of these rare allusions are clustered in the first chapter of Luke:

> In Luke 1:15 John the Baptist is presented as a Samson-like Nazirite (Judg 13:4) . . . . Luke 1:31 compares Mary to Samson's mother, who also received an angelic visitation announcing her pregnancy. Luke 1:42 compares the blessedness of Mary with that of Jael, the woman who killed Sisera (Judg 5:24).[2]

Block points out that the writer of Hebrews, in a famous chapter cataloging people who believed God, holds up the faith of some OT judges as exemplary (11:32). At least in certain moments of action against enemies of Israel, God's judges trusted in God. But often the

---

1. Block, *Judges/Ruth*, 69.
2. Block, *Judges/Ruth*, 69–70.

judges exhibited character and behavior that was offensive to God and ruinous to Israel.[3]

Luke's parallel of the book of Judges in Luke 13:34—19:44 does not take an overall interpretive position regarding the judges, whether positive or negative.[4] By imitating only selected features of the book of Judges instead of imitating cohesive judge-deliverer stories, Luke concerns himself with a larger truth: God's great deliverer has come.

DISTINCT THEMATIC PARALLELS

Features in the second half of Luke's journey narrative parallel similar or identical features in the book of Judges. The first half of the journey narrative displayed parallels to Moses from the book of Numbers as described above in chapter 3. The journey's second half, Luke 13:34—19:44, records parallels to the book of Judges. Thematic features from stories of these deliverers thickly pepper Luke 13:34—19:44.

Paralleled judges/journey features appear in many varieties: identical words, shared themes or concepts, similar movements of plot (on a small scale), thematic conversions, and dimensional similarities. By thematic conversions I mean, for example, a literal word paralleled by its metaphor, a specific word or theme paralleled by a generalized use of that word or theme, or an act in Judges paralleled (briefly) in Luke by a moral appraisal of that type of behavior. Dimensional similarities are correspondences of scope, quantity, distance, or topography. Features in Judges persistently parallel features in Luke 13:34—19:44 in the same position in the respective sequences of episodes.

Following are some of the more striking parallels between Judges and Luke's journey narrative:

---

3. Block, *Judges/Ruth*, 70.

4. Many of the Lukan imitations can be interpreted to take a dark view of the Judges model, but not consistently so. For example, the book of Judges celebrates the death of Sisera (4:17–21; 5:24–27), but the echo in Luke celebrates the life of the prodigal son and brother (15:23–32).

Kings, Deliverers, and Prophets in Luke's Journey Narrative

Judges	Luke
As a consequence for Israelite apostasy to other gods, the Lord allowed some nations to remain in the land: Philistines, Canaanites, Sidonians, Hittites, Amorites, Perezzites, Hivites, and Jebusites (3:3–6).	As a consequence for such snubs, the host demands a servant to "bring in the poor, the crippled, the blind, and the lame" (14:21), and to "Go out to the roads and lanes, and compel people to come in" (14:23).
So "the hand of the Lord was against them for evil, just as the Lord said and just as the Lord swore to them, and he afflicted them very much" (2:15).	"I tell you, none of those who were invited will taste my banquet" (14:24).
"I will show you the man whom you are seeking" (22). On the floor they found Sisera "thrown dead" (4:22).	"This brother of yours was dead, and has come to life; he was lost and has been found" (15:32).
Gideon asks the angel, "By what shall I save Israel?" (6:15).	The manager asks himself, "What will I do" to be welcomed into homes (16:3–4)?
Gideon blacklists seventy-seven rulers and elders of Succoth (8:14).	"If the same person sins against you seven times a day" and repents seven times, "you must forgive" (17:4).
Philistines "gouged out his eyes" (16:21).	"A blind man was sitting by the roadside begging" (18:35).
"The ambush rose up and deployed against Gibeah, and the ambush poured out, and they struck the city with the edge of the sword" (38). Israelite soldiers enter the city, annihilating every living thing and burning the city. Then Israel burns all the cities of Benjamin. Finally, the Israelites slaughter people and destroy the town of Jabesh-Gilead (20:36—21:25).	"The days will come upon you, when your enemies will set up ramparts around you, and hem you in on every side. They will crush you to the ground, you and your children within you" (19:43–44).

All striking parallels shown above also appear in our full catalog of sequential parallels starting on page 57.

In addition to the striking parallels listed above, four short segments of Luke 13:34—19:44 parallel short segments of Judges

Luke's Parallels of Judges as Deliverers

by compact clusters of parallels, where a few verses of Luke closely echo just a few verses of Judges.

Judg 1:22–26, depicted by Luke 14:1–6

Spies kept watch to gather intelligence against the city of Bethel (23).	Pharisees were watching Jesus carefully (14:1).
The narrator provides the demonstrative particle to prompt readers to imagine what the spies saw: "Look (*idou*), a man was going from the city" (24).	The narrator provides the demonstrative particle to prompt readers to imagine what the Pharisees and Jesus saw: "Just then (*idou*), in front of him, there was a man . . ." (2).*
After obtaining the intelligence that they needed, "the man, however, and his family they released" (25).	Jesus "took him and healed him, and sent him away" (4).

*At Luke 14:2, the RSV and ESV translate *idou* as "behold."

Judg 8:22–35, traced by Luke 17:7–19

Because God delivered Israel by the hand of Gideon, people say, "Rule us . . . because you have saved us from the hand of Midian" (22). Gideon answers, "I will not rule . . . the Lord will rule" (23).	"Do you thank the slave for doing what was commanded?" (9).
"The sons of Israel did not remember the Lord God that rescued them from the hand of all those oppressing them from all around" (34).	"Was none of them found to return and give praise to God except this foreigner?" (18).
"They did not show mercy" to the house of Gideon. They had no respect for "all the good that he did with Israel" (35).	"Jesus, Master, have mercy on us!" (13).

Judg 13:1–25, imitated by Luke 18:15–21

A man and his wife closely question an angel about their promised child (13:1–21).	Jesus rebukes his disciples for telling moms to keep their infants away from Jesus (18:15–17).

Manoah asks for the messenger's name (17). The messenger questions Manoah's motive, refuses to provide the name, allowing only that the name is "wondrous" (18).	A ruler calls Jesus "good." Jesus questions the ruler's motive and insists that the virtue "good" be applied only to God (18–19).
The messenger repeats for Manoah some of God's commands regarding the child, that it be raised under Nazirite rules (13–14).	Jesus lists commandments from the second tablet of the Law. The ruler claims that "I have kept all these since my youth" (21).

Judg 17:1–13, imitated by Luke 19:1–10

"There was a man from the hill country of Ephraim, and his name was Micah" (17:1).	"He entered Jericho.... A man was there named Zacchaeus" (19:1).
From a hoard of 1,100 pieces of silver, the man's mother gives him 200 pieces (17:2–5).	"He was a chief tax collector and was rich" (1).
"The man went . . . to sojourn wherever he might find a place" (8, 9).	"He ran ahead and climbed a sycamore tree" (4).
"Stay with me" (10).	"'I must stay at your house today.' So he hurried down and was happy to welcome him" (6).
"I will give you ten pieces of silver by the day and a garment of clothes and whatever you need for your living" (10).	"Half of my possessions, Lord, I will give to the poor; and if I have defrauded anyone of anything, I will pay back four times as much" (8).
"The Levite went and began to sojourn with the man. And the young man became to him like one of his sons" (11).	"Today salvation has come to this house, because he too is a son of Abraham" (9).

These four compact clusters of parallels also appear in our full catalog of sequential parallels below.

In sum, Luke organizes parallels to twenty-one narrative chapters of Judges in only six chapters of his Gospel. Whether in shorter or longer pieces of text, Luke echoes many features of the book of Judges in the last half of his journey narrative.

Luke's Parallels of Judges as Deliverers

LUKE'S PARALLELS OF JUDGES 1:1– 21:25 TO LUKE 13:34–19:44

We now fully trace parallels from the book of Judges in Luke's journey narrative, following the LXX of Judges as the model. In an imitation of judge-deliverers from the book of Judges, Luke 13:34–35 serves *both* as an essential middle block of journey text *and* as a journey bookend text.[5] *As a bookend text*, Luke 13:34–35 connects to the finish of Jesus' journey, and may be read there as the *beginning of the end* of the journey. As a middle block of Jesus' journey in the Third Gospel, Luke 13:34–35 imitates text at the beginning of the OT book of Judges, as seen in the table immediately below.

Judg 1:1–21, imitated by Luke 13:34–35	
The anachronistically used city name "Jerusalem (*Ierousalēm*)," instead of "Jebus," occurs four times in these twenty-two verses (1:7, 8, 21, 22).	The city name, "Jerusalem (*Ierousalēm*)," occurs three times in tight sequence (13:33–34).
On the way back to Jerusalem where he will be put to death, Adonibezek admits with prophetic clarity, "Just as I have done, thus God has repaid me" (7).	Ignoring Herod's death threat, Jesus declares, "It is impossible for a prophet to be killed outside of Jerusalem" (33).
Achsah "murmured and cried" to her father (14).	Jesus utters a lament over Jerusalem (34–35).
Achsah wisely makes advance arrangements for her new household in the arid south (14–15*).	"I desired to gather your children together as a hen gathers her brood under her wings" (34).
Achsah wants "a blessing" as she is sent off in marriage (15).	Jerusalem will not see Jesus until they are ready to bless him: "'Blessed is the one who comes in the name of the Lord'" (35).

*As proposed by Block, *Judges/Ruth*, 95–96.

---

5. See Appendix 1 for a more detailed explanation.

Judg 1:22–26, depicted by Luke 14:1–6

Spies kept watch to gather intelligence against the city of Bethel (1:23).	Pharisees were watching Jesus carefully (14:1).
The narrator provides the demonstrative particle to prompt readers to imagine what the spies saw: "Look (*idou*), a man was going from the city" (24).	The narrator provides the demonstrative particle to prompt readers to imagine what the Pharisees and Jesus saw: "Just then, in front of him (*idou*), there was a man . . ." (2).*
After obtaining the intelligence that they needed, "the man . . . and his family they released" (25).	Jesus "took him and healed him, and sent him away" (4).

*At Luke 14:2, the RSV and ESV translate *idou* as "behold."

Judg 1:27—3:6, intimated by Luke 14:7–35

"The Amorites forced the sons of Dan into the mountainous region, because they did not permit them to go down to the valley" (1:34).	"Sit down at the lowest place, so that when your host comes, he may say to you, 'Friend, move up higher'" (10).
The Lord "brought you out of Egypt and led you to the land (known as a land flowing with milk and honey)" (2:1; see Exod 3:17).	"Someone gave a great dinner and invited many" (16).
"You harkened not to my voice since you have done these things" (2).	But "they all alike began to make excuses," supposedly busy with a field, or oxen, or a wife. "Accept my regrets." "I cannot come" (18–20).
Israel "provoked the Lord" (13), making him "angered with wrath" (14, 20).	"The owner of the house became angry" (21).
So "the hand of the Lord was against them for evil, just as the Lord said and just as the Lord swore to them, and he afflicted them very much" (2:15).	"I tell you, none of those who were invited will taste my dinner" (24).
The Lord tested Israel whether "they will keep the way of the Lord" (22), "whether they would obey the commandments of the Lord" (3:4).	Whoever does not hate his own life (26), carry the cross (27), and give up all that he has (33), "and follow me cannot be my disciple" (27).

Luke's Parallels of Judges as Deliverers

"I . . . led you to the land (*eis tēn gēn*) that I swore to your fathers" (2:1).

"Salt is good . . ." (34).

But "you shall not make a covenant with the one who dwells in this land (*eis tēn gēn tautēn*)" (2). "They turned away swiftly" (17).

". . . but if salt has lost its taste, . . ." (34).

The Lord compassionately raised up judges to deliver Israel from the oppressor, but soon Israel turned away again and corrupted themselves (18–19).

". . . how can its saltiness be restored?" (34)

Therefore, the Lord will not drive out the nations living "in the land (*en tē gē*)" (21).

It is not fit "for the soil (*eis gēn*)" (35).

"But you harkened not to my voice" (2). They turned away "from the way that their fathers listened to the words of the Lord" (17). "They did not listen to my voice" (20).

"Let anyone with ears to hear, listen!" (35)

Judg 3:7–31, countered by Luke 15:1–10

"The Lord raised up a deliverer" (3:9), who delivered Israel.

"Which one of you" goes "after the one that is lost until he finds it" (15:4).

The Lord raises up another deliverer, Ehud, who "made for himself a two-edged sword" (16), and presented King Eglon of Moab with gifts (gold? silver?) (17).

"What woman having ten silver coins . . ?" (8).

The dagger penetrated deeply, disappeared in the fat, and remained in the king's belly (21–22).

". . . if she loses one of them . . ." (8).

Action takes place in a "most private summer room upstairs" (20).

Imagined action takes place in "the house" (8).

Eglon's servants come to the outer room, wait patiently until they are ashamed, then unlock the inner room, and find Eglon dead on the floor (24–25).

"She calls together her friends and neighbors, saying, 'Rejoice with me, for I have found the coin that I had lost.'" (9)

Kings, Deliverers, and Prophets in Luke's Journey Narrative

Judg 4:1–24, matched by Luke 15:11–32

Sisera's forces fall in battle, and Sisera desperately runs on foot for his life (4:15).	The younger son "began to be in need" (14).
Sisera commits himself into a local resident's protection, hiding in Jael's tent (17–18).	"He went and hired himself out to one of the citizens of that country" (15).
"Give me a little water to drink." "She opened the wineskin of milk and gave him a drink" (19).	"A severe famine took place throughout that country" (14).
"I will show you the man whom you are seeking" (22). On the floor they found Sisera "thrown dead" (22).	"This brother of yours was dead, and has come to life; he was lost and has been found" (32).

Luke excludes the song of Deborah and Barak (Judg 5:1–31) from his imitation, using only narrative portions of Judges. Luke does likewise with blocks of legal statutes in Numbers.

Judg 6:1–24, paralleled by Luke 16:1–13

Midian and Amalek maraud the land of Israel (6:3) and "destroy their fruits" (6:4).	"There was a rich man rich man who had a manager" who "was squandering his property" (16:1).
An angel ironically states, "The Lord is with you, mighty one of power" (12) "Go in this strength of yours" (14).	The manager admits to himself, "I am not strong enough to dig" (3).
Gideon complains that the Lord "has cast us out" (13).	The manager worries, "When I am dismissed as manager . . ." (4).
Gideon asks the angel, "By what shall I save Israel?" (15).	The manager asks himself, "What will I do" to be welcomed into homes (3–4)?
In gratitude for the Lord's promised provision, Gideon presents a thank offering of meat, bread, and broth to the angel of the Lord (19–21).	The manager tries to provide for himself by ingratiating to himself the rich man's debtors who owe the rich man large quantities of oil and wheat (5–7).
The Lord affirms, "Peace be to you, do not fear; you shall not die" (23).	Jesus teaches that godly discipleship of wealth bears upon entry to eternal life (9–13).

Luke's Parallels of Judges as Deliverers

Judg 6:25–40, echoed by Luke 16:14–18

The Lord says, "Take down the altar of Baal that belongs to your father; also, the sacred grove by it you shall destroy. And you shall build an altar to the Lord your God" (6:25–26).	"What is prized by human beings is an abomination in the sight of God" (16:15).
Gideon's father, owner of the altar and grove, shows a changed heart by supporting Gideon's actions (31).	People forcefully enter (or "are urged to enter") the kingdom of God (16).
Men of the city want to kill Gideon because he desecrated Baal and worshipped the Lord instead (30).	Divorce with remarriage is adultery (18).
Joash threatens the life of any who contend for Baal instead of the Lord (31).	Marrying a divorced woman is adultery (18).

Judg 7:1—8:3, countered by Luke 16:19–31

Excess resources: "The people with you" (7:2) are too numerous. "Still the people is plentiful" (4).	Excess consumption: "There was a rich man who was dressed in purple and fine linen and who feasted sumptuously every day" (19).
"Anyone who laps" like "the dog laps" (5).	"Even the dogs would come and lick his sores" (21).
Put to one side "everyone who bows upon his knee to drink" (5).	"Send Lazarus to dip the tip of his finger in water and cool my tongue" (24).
The camp of Gideon is on a hilltop, and the Midianite camp is before them in the valley. The Lord commands Gideon to make a normally suicidal trip down to the Midianites (8–12).	"A great chasm has been fixed, so that those who might want to pass from here to you cannot do so, and no one can cross from there to us" (26).
Gideon "sent messengers" to three tribes of Israel (24).	"Send him to my father's house— for I have five brothers" (27).
"They argued against (Gideon) intensely" (8:1).	From Hades, the rich man argues with father Abraham: "Then, father, I beg you . . ." (27). "No, father Abraham; but . . ." (30).

Kings, Deliverers, and Prophets in Luke's Journey Narrative

Judg 8:4–21, imitated by Luke 17:1–6

Rulers of Succoth and Penuel refuse to help Gideon's men, and they taunt Gideon instead (8:5–6).	"Occasions for stumbling are bound to come, but woe to anyone by whom they come!" (17:1).
Gideon warns them that their lives will be forfeit for their failure to help in time of need (7).	"If another disciple sins, you must rebuke the offender" (3).
Gideon blacklists seventy-seven rulers and elders of Succoth (14).	"If the same person sins against you seven times a day" and repents seven times, "you must forgive" (4).

Judg 8:22–35, traced by Luke 17:7–19

Because God delivered Israel by the hand of Gideon, people say, "Rule us . . . because you have saved us from the hand of Midian" (8:22). Gideon answers, "I will not rule . . . the Lord will rule" (23).	"Do you thank the slave for doing what was commanded?" (17:9).
"The sons of Israel did not remember the Lord God that rescued them from the hand of all those oppressing them from all around" (34).	"Was none of them found to return and give praise to God except this foreigner?" (18).
"They did not show mercy" to the house of Gideon. They had no respect for "all the good that he did with Israel" (35).	"Jesus, Master, have mercy on us!" (13).

Judg 9:1–57, intimated by Luke 17:20–37

Abimelech exhorts men of Shechem to make him master over them. All the men of Shechem and the house of Beth-millo come together and make Abimelech king (9:1–6).	Pharisees ask Jesus "when the kingdom of God was coming" (17:20).
What "is good for you, that . . . one man be master over you? Remember that I am your bone and your flesh" (2).	"You will long to see one of the days of the Son of Man" (22).

Luke's Parallels of Judges as Deliverers

Abimelech hires attendants who "went following him" (4).	"Do not go, do not set off in pursuit" (23).
Jotham prophesies, "Let fire go out" to "devour" (20).	"For as lightning flashes and lights up the sky from one side to the other, so will the Son of Man be in his day" (24).
"God sent an evil spirit" to confuse, subvert, and destroy Abimelech and his supporters (23).	"But first he must endure much suffering and be rejected by this generation" (25).
Gaal and his brothers "went out into a field and gathered their vines; and they trod them" and made wine. They ate and drank and cursed Abimelech (27).	"They were eating and drinking" (27, 28).
Abimelech's people strike down all who work in the fields (42–44).	"Anyone in the field must not turn back" (31).
Abimelech kills the people of the city, razes the city, and sows it with salt (45).	"Remember Lot's wife" (who turned into a pillar of salt) (32).
About a thousand men and women shelter from Abimelech's wrath in the Tower of Shechem, but are burned alive when Abimelech sets the tower on fire (47–49).	"Those who try to make their life secure will lose it" (33).
"One woman threw a fragment of millstone at Abimelech's head, and it broke his skull" (53).	"There will be two women grinding meal together; one will be taken and the other left" (34).
Abimelech dies and his militia see their dead leader (55).	"Where the corpse is, there the vultures will gather" (37).

Judg 10:1—11:26, imitated by Luke 18:1-8

Israel "continued to do evil before the Lord" (10:6), worshipping other gods. "The king of the sons of Ammon did not hearken to the words of Jephthah" (11:28).	"There was a judge who neither feared God nor had respect for people" (18:2).
Israel "abandoned the Lord and did not serve him" (10:6). "You deserted me and served other gods" (13).	"There was a widow" (3).

63

But the Lord's "soul was diminished by the suffering (*en kopō*) of Israel" (16).	"Though I have no fear of God and no respect for anyone, yet because this widow keeps bothering me (*parechein moi kopon*), I will grant her justice" (5).
The Ammonite king presses Jephthah to "return" territory east of the Jordan that God had given to Israel. (11:13) Jephthah argues that for "three hundred years" it belonged to Israel, so why claim it now for Ammon (26)?	"Will not God grant justice to his chosen ones . . . ? Will he delay long in helping them?" (7).

Judg 11:27—12:15, imaged by Luke 18:9-14

"I have not sinned against you" (11:27).	"I am not like other people: thieves, rogues, adulterers, or even like this tax collector" (18:11).
Israel's Jephthah makes an Amorite vow to burn a human thank-offering. (30–31)*	Not actually praying to God, the Pharisee brags, "I fast twice a week; I give a tenth of all my income" (12).
Jephthah's daughter accepts her fate, "Father, do to me in the way you have said" (36).	"The tax collector . . . would not even look up to heaven," but said, "God, be merciful to me, a sinner" (13).
She prepares to die by finding a remote place to wail (37–38).	The tax collector "stood far off" and "was beating his breast" (13).
Ephraimite leaders are offended that Jephthah did not mobilize them to fight against Ammon. Ephraimites therefore threaten to incinerate Jephthah in his own home (12:1).	"All who exalt themselves . . ." (14).
In response, Jephthah and the Gileadites struck down "forty-two thousand" Ephraimites (6).	". . . will be humbled" (14).
*For more on this insight, see Block, *Judge/Ruth*, 365–69.	

Luke's Parallels of Judges as Deliverers

Judg 13:1-25, imitated by Luke 18:15-21

An angel, a man, and his wife interact regarding a future, prophesied child (13:1-21).	Jesus rebukes the disciples for blocking mothers who bring their infants for Jesus' blessing (18:15-17).
Manoah asks for the messenger's name (17). The messenger questions Manoah's motive, refuses to provide the name (18), allowing only that the name is "wondrous" (18).	A ruler calls Jesus "good." Jesus questions the ruler's motive and insists that the virtue "good" be applied only to God (18-19).
The messenger repeats for Manoah some of God's commands regarding the child, that it be raised under Nazirite rigor (13-14).	Jesus lists commandments from the second tablet of the Law. The ruler claims that "I have kept all these since my youth" (21).

Judg 14:1—15:20, represented by Luke 18:22-30

"I saw a woman . . . ; now get her for me for a wife" (14:2).	"There is still one thing lacking" (18:22).
Samson's parents object that he is spurning the daughters of his brothers, and spurning any "woman from all my people" for this non-Israelite woman (3).	Jesus teaches on leaving "house or wife or brothers or parents or children, for the sake of the kingdom of God" (29-30).
Philistines were "masters in Israel" at that time, but the Lord "desired vengeance" on them (4).	"What is impossible for mortals is possible with God" (26).
Samson marries but continues to live at home with his parents while making visits to his current wife (14:5-9; 15:1).	Those who leave "house or wife or brothers or parents or children" for the sake of the kingdom of God will "get back very much more" (29-30).

Judg 16:1-31, imitated by Luke 18:31-43

Delilah delivers Samuel to the Philistines (16:4-20).	The Son of Man "will be handed over to the Gentiles" (18:32).
"'Call Samson from the prison house and let him sport before us.' And they summoned Samson from the prison house, and he sported before them, and they struck him" (25).	The Son of Man "will be mocked and insulted and spat upon" (32).

Kings, Deliverers, and Prophets in Luke's Journey Narrative

Samson "did not know that the Lord had departed from him" (20).	"They understood nothing about all of these things; in fact, what he said was hidden from them, and they did not grasp what was said" (34).
Philistines "gouged out his eyes" (21).	"A blind man was sitting by the roadside begging" (35).
"Adonai, O Lord, remember me now, I pray, and strengthen me yet again this one time, O God" (28).	"Jesus, Son of David, have mercy on me!" (38, 39). "Lord, let me see again" (41).
"The house fell upon the rulers and upon all the people with him" (30).	"All the people, when they saw it, praised God" (43).

Judg 17:1–13, imitated by Luke 19:1–10

"There was a man from the hill country of Ephraim, and his name was Micah" (17:1).	"He entered Jericho . . . A man was there named Zacchaeus" (19:1).
From a hoard of 1,100 pieces of silver, the man's mother gives him 200 pieces (17:2–5).	"He was a chief tax collector and was rich" (1).
"The man went . . . to sojourn wherever he might find a place" (8, 9).	"He ran ahead and climbed a sycamore tree" (4).
"Stay with me" (10).	"'I must stay at your house today.' So he hurried down and was happy to welcome him" (6).
"I will give you ten pieces of silver by the day and a garment of clothes and whatever you need for your living" (10).	"Half of my possessions, Lord, I will give to the poor; and if I have defrauded anyone of anything, I will pay back four times as much" (8).
"The Levite went and began to sojourn with the man. And the young man became to him like one of his sons" (11).	"Today salvation has come to this house, because he too is a son of Abraham" (9).

Judg 18:1–31, imitated by Luke 19:11–27

"In those days there was no king in Israel" (18:1, 31).	The people "supposed that the kingdom of God was to appear immediately" (19:11).

Luke's Parallels of Judges as Deliverers

"The tribe of Dan was seeking for themselves an inheritance to inhabit" (1).

"The sons of Dan sent from their region five men" to "spy out the land and to explore it" (2). "Go and explore the land" (2).

Micah and his men "shouted and overtook the sons of Dan" (22), wanting the graven image and the priest back (24).

"Let not your voice be heard with us" on pain of death (25).

"A nobleman went to a distant country to get royal power for himself and then return" (12).

"He summoned ten of his slaves, and gave them ten pounds, and said to them, 'Do business with these until I come back'" (13).

"But the citizens of his country hated him and sent a delegation after him, saying, 'We do not want this man to rule over us'" (14).

"As for these enemies of mine, who did not want me to be king over them—bring them here and slaughter them in my presence" (27).

Judg 19:1–21, countered by Luke 19:28–40

A Levite, his concubine, and his servant "arose and went as far as Jebus (that is, Jerusalem)" (19:10).

The Levite's group "turned aside there in Gibeah" (15).

"There was no one" offering hospitality (15, 18).

The travelers are questioned: "Where are you going and from where have you come?" (17).

We have "no lack of anything" (19). They even brought their own fodder for the donkeys (19).

"Peace to you" (20).

"He went on ahead, going up to Jerusalem" (19:28).

"Go into the village ahead of you" (30).

If "anyone" asks you . . . (31).

The travelers are questioned: "Why?" (31, 33).

"The Lord needs" the colt (31, 34).

"Peace in heaven, and glory in the highest heaven!" (38).

For the end of the Judges story, we might expect that we would, according to Luke's pattern in final echoes of David and Moses, hear echoes of Judges 20–21 in Luke 13:33–35 (in its bookend role) as well as Luke 19:41–44. In the concluding two chapters of Judges, however, we have not climax, but anti-climax as tribes of Israel attack one another. In this light, it appears that the appropriate bookend imitating text in Luke is 13:31–33, where threat of death and questions of resistance or flight set the tone.

Judg 20:12–35, imitated by Luke 13:31–33

"The tribes of Israel sent men" (20:12). "Hand over the men, sons of lawlessness . . . and we shall put them to death" (13).	"Some Pharisees came and said to him, 'Get away from here, for Herod wants to kill you'" (13:31).
"That day" (21). "The second day" (24, 25). "Tomorrow" (28). "The third day" (30).	"I am casting out demons and performing cures today and tomorrow, and on the third day I finish my work. Yet today, tomorrow, and the next day I must be on my way" (32–33).

Judg 20:36—21:25, echoed by Luke 19:41-44

Israel plants troops in hiding to ambush Gibeah. Fighters of Israel give ground to draw Benjamite fighters away from Gibeah, in order to spring the ambush (20:36–40).	"But now they are hidden from your eyes" (19:42).
"The ambush rose up and deployed against Gibeah, and the ambush poured out, and they struck the city with the edge of the sword" (38). Israelite soldiers enter the city, annihilating every living thing and burning the city. Then Israel burns all the cities of Benjamin. Finally, the Israelites slaughter people and destroy the town of Jabesh-Gilead (20:36—21:25).	"The days will come upon you, when your enemies will set up ramparts around you, and hem you in on every side. They will crush you to the ground, you and your children within you" (43–44).

Luke matches episodes of the Jesus tradition to a set of sequential features from the book of Judges, making Luke 13:31—19:44 parallel *God's deliverers in Judges*. The evangelist follows the same procedure as he did with the book of Numbers, where he matches features of journey episodes to features of Moses the deliverer. Not only does Luke accomplish this unique literary-theological project

Luke's Parallels of Judges as Deliverers

regarding God's deliverers, but Luke also uses the very same Jesus episodes that he arranged into a thematic reflection of David's ascendancy from 1–2 Kingdoms. Further, as will be shown in the following chapter, Luke matches a set of features from the same gospel episodes as echoes of a sequential set of features from the ministries of Elijah and Elisha from the books of 3 and 4 Kingdoms.

> What's up, old baldhead! Out of our way, Skinhead!
>
> 2 KGS 2:23 (*MSG*)

> He pays even greater attention to you, down to the last detail—even numbering the hairs on your head! So don't be intimidated by all this bully talk.
>
> LUKE 12:7 (*MSG*)

5

Luke's Echoes of the Prophets Elijah and Elisha

BEGINNING ABOUT 1980, THOMAS Brodie began publishing a series of journal articles claiming that Luke produced imitations of the Old Testament prophet Elijah's life in portions of the Third Gospel, including an imitation at the beginning of Luke's journey narrative (2 Kgs 1:1—2:6, imitated by Luke 9.51–56).[1] Our study of the journey narrative also hears echoes of the Elijah (and Elisha) narratives in Luke. While other portions of Luke's Gospel may perhaps echo themes from the lives of those two great northern prophets, the Lukan journey narrative (9:51—19:44) sequentially echoes themes from 3 Kingdoms 19:1 to 4 Kingdoms 17:23.[2]

---

1. Brodie, "Departure for Jerusalem," 96–109.
2. Our reader should keep in mind that the "1 Kings" and "2 Kings" of Hebrew-based English Bibles are called "3 Kingdoms" and "4 Kingdoms" in the Greek-based *Lexham English Septuagint*. For brevity, we shorten "Kingdoms" to "Kgdms."

Luke's Echoes of the Prophets Elijah and Elisha

DISTINCT THEMATIC ECHOES

The clearest echoes of Elijah's ministry in Jesus' journey are heard just before and just within the beginning of Luke's journey narrative. First, Elijah's departure from Jezebel's Samaria follows a mountaintop epiphany (3 Kgdms 18:17-40) in which the fire of God falls from heaven to vindicate the name of the real God and to vindicate the role of Elijah as God's servant (36, 39). Likewise, Jesus' departure from Galilee, narrated in the final lines of Luke 9, follows a mountaintop epiphany (9:28-36) in which God's voice from heaven identifies a transfigured Jesus as "my Son, my Chosen" (36). Elijah stands on the mountaintop in conversation with Jesus (30). The paragraphs before the beginning of Jesus' journey in Luke 9 echo the chapter before Elijah's journey in 3 Kingdoms.

Second, another striking parallel between Elijah's story and Jesus' story occurs not long after both journeys begin. God gives Elijah an understudy and future replacement in the person of Elisha. In 3 Kingdoms 19:15-21, Elisha is plowing in the field. Elijah comes by and claims Elisha for prophetic ministry, and Elisha asks to make a proper farewell to his parents before joining Elijah. The farewell event takes place, and then Elisha follows Elijah. In Luke 9:61-62, by contrasting tone and imagery, a new follower of Jesus asks to return home to say his farewell, but Jesus refuses, likening discipleship to resolute, focused field-plowing, allowing no distractions. These eye-catching parallels come near the beginning of both narratives. Such clear echoes of Elijah's ministry in Jesus' journey prompt readers to consider whether Jesus' ministry might in some way parallel that of Elijah in the respective series of episodes that follow.[3]

Elijah is the first prophet echoed in Luke's journey narrative, but not the only one. Elijah dies in 4 Kingdoms 2:1-6, and echoes of Elijah suddenly cease at the end of Luke 11. But the ministry of Elijah continues in the acts of Elisha, and so also continues Luke's imitative parallel of themes from 4 Kingdoms. Later, 4 Kingdoms recounts Elisha's death (13:14-21, echoed by Luke 17:20-21),

---

3. Elijah and Moses appear with the transfigured Jesus (Luke 9:30-33). These men appeared "in glory" (31). The three confer as if equal in standing, except that God's voice speaks, clarifying that Jesus is God's son (35).

yet the Lukan journey imitations continue yet further. The end of Jesus' journey in Luke 19 parallels the death of the Northern Kingdom, "Israel," when Assyria devastates it (4 Kgdms 17:5–23, echoed by Luke 19:41–44). The story of the Northern Kingdom concludes in a summary of why God abandoned Israel to Assyria. Likewise, Luke's journey narrative ends with a lament warning Jerusalem about its own spiritual intransigence.

LUKE'S ECHOES OF 3 KINGDOMS 19:1—4 KINGDOMS 17:23 IN LUKE 9:51—19:44

We now list echoes from the Elijah and Elisha narratives (portions of 3 and 4 Kgdms) in Luke 9:51—19:44. As in Luke's parallels of Jesus to David's story and to Moses' story, Luke 13:31-33 serves two functions. *As a bookend text*, Luke 13:31-33 parallels certain features of Elijah's flight from Jezebel. Thus, Luke's imitation from 3 Kingdoms begins at Luke 13:31-33 and then it continues in 9:51–56.[4]

3 Kgdms 19:1-14, echoed by Luke 13:31-33 and 9:51-60

3 Kgdms 19:1-14	Luke 13:31-33 and 9:51-60
Jezebel announces that she will kill Elijah. (19:2)	Pharisees warn that "Herod wants to kill" Jesus, and that Jesus should leave right away. (13:31)
Jezebel swears that Elijah will die by "tomorrow" (2).	Jesus counters that he will continue his ministry "today and tomorrow, and the third day I finish my work. Yet today, tomorrow, and the next day I must be on my way" (32-33).
The Lord sent an angel (*angellos*) to prepare Elijah for his travel to Horeb. (5-7)	Jesus "sent messengers (*angelloi*) ahead of him . . . to make ready for him" (9:52).
"He fell asleep and slept there under the tree" (5).	"The Son of Man has nowhere to lay his head" (58).
Elijah journeys toward Horeb (the mountain of God). (8)	Jesus sets out on a journey to Jerusalem (Zion, the mountain of God). (51-53)

---

4. See Appendix 1 for a more detailed explanation.

Luke's Echoes of the Prophets Elijah and Elisha

In a preceding episode, Elijah calls on the Lord to send fire to consume the offering of the priests of Baal (18:36–38).	"Lord, do you want us to command fire to come down from heaven and consume them?" (54).
"I am zealous for the Lord Almighty" (19:14).	"I will follow you wherever you go" (57).

3 Kgdms 19:15–21, imitated by Luke 9:61–62

Elisha "was plowing with oxen" (19).	"No one who puts a hand to the plow and looks back is fit for the kingdom of God" (9:62).
"Let me kiss my father, and I will follow after you" (20).	"I will follow you, Lord; but let me first say farewell to those at my home" (61).

The chapter order of 3 Kingdoms in the LXX differs from that of 1 Kings in Hebrew: they are in reverse chapter order (3 Kgdms 20 = 1 Kings 21, and 3 Kgdms 21 = 1 Kings 20). Curiously, however, Luke follows the Hebrew Bible's chapter order. Luke echoes 3 Kingdoms 21 before he echoes 3 Kingdoms 20.

Some possible explanations for this might be: 1) Luke used a differently ordered Greek OT than that translated in the *Lexham English Septuagint*; (2) Luke knew the chapter order of the Hebrew Bible and preferred it over the chapter order of the Greek OT; or (3) Luke aligned his work to the Hebrew Bible in any questionable matters. We will follow the textual order recognized by Luke's parallels: 3 Kingdoms 21 followed by 3 Kingdoms 20.[5]

3 Kgdms 21:1–43 resonates in Luke 10:1–42

Ben-hadad gathered thirty-two kings and their armies to besiege Samaria (21:1).	"The Lord appointed seventy (two) others and sent them on ahead of him to every town and place where he himself intended to go" (10:1).

---

5. In the following table, "Syria" and "Aram/Arameans" are the same people, more clearly identified as Aram-Damascus.

Ben-hadad's servants will "search your house and the houses of your servants," taking "whatever" they want (6).	When you enter a house, stay there. "Do not move about from house to house." Eat and drink "whatever they provide" (7).
"If the dirt of Samaria is sufficient . . . for my infantry" (10).	"Even the dust of your town that clings to our feet, we wipe off in protest against you" (11).
They build a war palisade around Samaria (12).	Woes against named cities (13–15).
The forces of Samaria overwhelm the far larger Syrian army (19–20).	"Lord, in your name even the demons submit to us!" (17).
Ahab takes all remaining horses and chariots from the battlefield as spoils of war (21).	"I have given you authority to tread on snakes and scorpions, and over all the power of the enemy" (19).
Syrian advisors mistakenly believe that Israel's God is a "god of the mountains, but not a god of the deep valley" (23).	"No one knows who the Son is except the Father, or who the Father is except the Son and anyone to whom the Son chooses to reveal him" (22).
"The man of God came and said to the king of Israel, 'This is what the Lord says'" (28).	"Many prophets and kings desired to see what you see, but did not see it, and to hear what you hear, but did not hear it" (24).
How shall the Arameans regard "the Lord the God of Israel?" (28).	"You shall love the Lord your God with all your heart" (27).
Israel struck down many Syrian troops and a wall fell on many others, forcing the hapless king, Ben-hadad, into hiding (29–30).	A man "fell into the hands of robbers . . . leaving him half dead" (30).
"I know that the kings of Israel are merciful kings" (31). Ahab responds positively to the Syrians' plea for mercy (32–33).	When a Samaritan saw the wounded man lying in the road, "he was moved with pity" (33).
Ben-hadad flees and enters someone's house (30).	"Martha welcomed him into her home" (38).
Ahab allows that Ben-hadad "is my brother" (32).	Martha "had a sister named Mary" (39).
The defeated Ben-hadad is made to stand on the chariot with victorious King Ahab (33).	Mary "sat at the Lord's feet and listened to what he was saying" (39).

Luke's Echoes of the Prophets Elijah and Elisha

"The king of Israel departed, troubled and having failed" (43).

"Martha, Martha, you are worried and distracted by many things" (41).

Luke, having echoed features from 3 Kingdoms 21, now takes up 3 Kingdoms 20. He engages with the chapter order of the Hebrew Bible, rather than the chapter order of the LXX.

3 Kgdms 20:1-29, matched by Luke 11:1-28

"Give me your vineyard" (20:2) "Give" appears seven times in 2-6.	"Give us each day our daily bread" (11:3). "Give" appears eight times in 3-13.
Naboth refuses to give his vineyard (3).	A friend at first refuses to give bread (5-7).
Naboth will not give over what he has received from his "father" (3), or from his "fathers" (6).	"When you pray, say: Father" (1). "The heavenly Father (will) give . . . to those who ask him" (13).
Jezebel persists in acquiring the vineyard (5-14).	"Because of his persistence (the friend) will get up and give him whatever he needs" (8).
Naboth does not speak a blasphemy, but is charged with doing so (13).	They claim that Jesus "casts out demons by Beelzebul, the ruler of demons" (15).
Ahab regrets causing Naboth's death and grieves being the cause of it, but nevertheless takes possession of Naboth's property (16).	"Every kingdom divided against itself becomes a desert . . ." (17).
The Lord sends judgment on both Ahab and Jezebel (17-26).	". . . and house falls on house" (17).
"You have sold yourself pointlessly to do evil before the Lord to provoke him to anger" (20).	"Whoever is not with me is against me, and whoever does not gather with me scatters" (23).
Ahab let Jezebel lead him into evil, but his greater sin is leading Israel into idolatry with the gods of the Amorites (25-26).	A spirit "goes and brings seven other spirits more evil than itself." "The last state of that person is worse than the first" (26).
"Concerning the matter (*tou logou*), Ahab was so stupefied from the face of the Lord, that he went lamenting and tore his garment" (27).	Blessed are "those who hear the word of God (*ton logon*) and obey it" (28).

Kings, Deliverers, and Prophets in Luke's Journey Narrative

3 Kgdms 22:1-28, echoed by Luke 11:29-32

Jehoshephat wants Ahab to "consult the Lord" about war plans (22:5).	This evil generation "asks for a sign" (11:29).
"There is one man through which to consult the Lord" (8).	"No sign will be given to it except the sign of Jonah" (29).
"Jehoshaphat king of Judah came" (from Jerusalem in the South), apparently for a state visit (2).	"The queen of the South . . . came . . . to listen to the wisdom of Solomon" (31).
"Is there not here a (greater) prophet of the Lord that we may consult the Lord through him?" (7).	Someone "greater than (wise) Solomon is here" (31).
"Whatever the Lord says to me, I will speak these things" (14).	Someone "greater than Jonah (who would not at first preach God's message) is here" (32).

3 Kgdms 22:29-36, figured by Luke 11:33-36

"The king of Israel disguised himself and entered into the battle" (22:30).	"No one after lighting a lamp puts it in a cellar . . ." (11:33).
"When the rulers of the chariot teams saw that this one was not the king of Israel, they turned away from him" (33).	". . . but on the lampstand so that those who enter may see the light" (33).
"The battle reached a turning point on that day" (35).	Verse 34b-c is the *center or turning point* of the chiasm that makes up 33-36.
An arrow "struck the king of Israel between the lungs and between the breastplates" (34).	If your eye is not healthy, "your body is full of darkness. Therefore consider whether the light in you is not darkness" (34-35).
"The herald stood at the setting of the sun saying, 'Everyone to his own town, and to his own land, for the king has died'" (36-37a).	If your body has "no part of it in darkness, it will be full of light as when a lamp gives you light with its rays" (36).

In the pairing of 3 Kingdoms 22:35 and Luke 11:34b-c above, we find yet another approach that Luke takes in matching gospel resources to OT narrative for the sake of affirming truth about Jesus. Luke matches a turn in the narrative flow of 3 Kingdoms 22

Luke's Echoes of the Prophets Elijah and Elisha

("reached a turning point") with a middle turn in the chiastic literary flow of Jesus' teaching in Luke 11.[6]

3 Kgdms 22:37–51, countered by Luke 11:37–44

"They washed off the blood" (22:38). "The prostitutes washed in the blood" (38).	"The Pharisee was amazed to see that he did not first wash before dinner" (11:38).
"Only the high places he did not take away" (44).	"You Pharisees clean the outside of the cup and of the dish, but inside you are full of greed and wickedness" (39).
"He was buried in the city of David his father" (51).	"Woe to you! For you are like unmarked graves, and people walk over them without realizing it" (44).

3 Kgdms 22:52—4 Kgdms 1:18, imitated by Luke 11:45–52

"He provoked the Lord God of Israel just as all those who were before him" (22:54).	"You . . . approve of the deeds of your ancestors" (11:48).
Ahaziah sent messengers: "Go and inquire from Baal-zebub, god of Ekron" (4 Kgdms 1:2).	"You load people with burdens hard to bear" (46).
An angel of the Lord says to Elijah: "Arise! Come to a meeting of the messengers of Ahaziah" (3). The messengers return to Ahaziah with Elijah's message (5).	"I will send them prophets and apostles" (49).
Ahaziah sends a series of three companies of soldiers to apprehend Elijah (9, 11, 13).	Three "woes" to lawyers (46, 47, 52).

4 Kgdms 2:1–6, traced by Luke 11:53–54

"When the Lord brought up Elijah in the air and so into heaven" (2:1).	"When he went outside" (11:53).

---

6. See page 12.

Kings, Deliverers, and Prophets in Luke's Journey Narrative

Elisha pesters Elijah: "As the Lord lives and as your soul lives, cursed if I will leave you" (2, 4, 6). Sons of the prophets pester Elisha: "Do you know that today the Lord will remove your master from above your head?" (3, 5).	"The scribes and Pharisees began . . . to cross-examine him about many things" (53).

4 Kgdms 2:7–25, imitated by Luke 12:1–7

"Fifty men, sons of the prophets . . ." (7).	"The crowd gathered by the thousands . . ." (12:1).
". . . stood opposite them from a distance" (7).	". . . so that they trampled on one another" (12:1).
In private, Elisha asked, "May your spirit become twofold on me" (9). After Elijah's departure, "the sons of the prophets and those who were in Jericho," observing from a distance, said, "The spirit of Elijah has rested upon Elisha" (15).	"Nothing is covered up that will not be uncovered, and nothing secret that will not become known. Therefore whatever you have said in the dark will be heard in the light, and what you have whispered behind closed doors will be proclaimed from the housetops" (2–3).
"They urged him until he was ashamed" (17).	"Do not fear" people (4–5).
"Go up, bald man! Go up!" (23).	"Even the hairs on your head are all counted" (7).
God's prophet "cursed them in the name of the Lord. Look, two bears came out from the forest and tore apart forty-two children from them" (24).	"Do not be afraid; you are of more value than many sparrows" (7).

4 Kgdms 3:1–27, echoed by Luke 12:8–40

King Joram of Israel "did evil in the eyes of the Lord" and "clung to the sin of Jeroboam son of Nebat" (3:2–3).	"Everyone who acknowledges me before others, the Son of Man also will acknowledge before the angels of God; but whoever denies me before others will be denied before the angels of God" (12:8–9).

Luke's Echoes of the Prophets Elijah and Elisha

"The king of Israel; Jehoshaphat, king of Judah; and the king of Edom" go to consult Elisha (12).

"The word is with him" (12). "Now bring me harpists" (15). "As the harpist played, the hand of the Lord came upon him" (15).

Mesha of Moab gives annual tribute of 100,000 lambs and wool (see MT) of 100,000 rams to Israel's Ahab (4).

But Ahab dies and is succeeded by his son Joram, which offers Mesha of Moab an opening to rebel, thus cutting off a supply of lambs and wool to Israel (5).

"There was not water for the encampment or the livestock" (9).

King Joram complains, "Has the Lord indeed called the three kings . . . to give them into the hand of Moab?" (10).

Unless he can see the face of the king of Judah, Elisha will not entertain Joram's plea for help (14).

"This brook will be filled with water, and you . . . will drink" (17).

"This is also a light matter in the eyes of the Lord. He will give Moab into your hand" (18).

"It happened early in the morning" (20). "They rose up early, and the sun was rising on the water" (22).

"'Now to the spoils, Moab.' They entered into the fort of Israel" (23–24).

"When they bring you before . . . the rulers, and the authorities, do not worry about how you are to defend yourselves or what you are to say . . ." (11).

". . . for the Holy Spirit will teach you at that very hour what you ought to say" (12).

"The land of a rich man produced abundantly" (16).

"Do not worry about your life, what you will eat, or about your body, what you will wear. For life is more than food, and the body more than clothing" (22–23). (See also 24–28.)

"Do not keep striving for . . . what you are to drink" (29).

"For it is the nations of the world that strive after all these things, and your Father knows that you need them" (30).

"Strive for his kingdom . . ." (31).

". . . and these things will be given to you as well" (31).

"It is your Father's good pleasure to give you the kingdom" (32).

"If he comes . . . near dawn" (38).

"If the owner of the house had known at what hour the thief was coming, he would not have let his house be broken into" (39).

Kings, Deliverers, and Prophets in Luke's Journey Narrative

4 Kgdms 4:1–7, represented by Luke 12:41–48

"Your servant, my husband died, and you know that the servant was one who feared the Lord" (4:1).	"Who then is the faithful and prudent manager . . . ?" (12:42).
"The moneylender has come to take my two sons for his own slaves" (1).	"Blessed is that slave whom his master will find at work when he arrives" (43).
"Nothing belongs to your servant—nothing other than olive oil" (2).	"He will put that one in charge of all his possessions" (44).
"Ask for vessels . . . from all the neighbors, empty vessels. Don't skimp. . . . Enter . . . shut the door . . . pour into these jars . . . take up the full ones" (4).	"That slave who knew what his master wanted . . ." (47; see also 43).
"Go and sell the oil. You can repay your interest, and you and your sons can live on the remaining oil" (7).	"From everyone to whom much has been given, much will be required" (48).

4 Kgdms 4:8–37, imitated by Luke 12:49–59

A son complains to his father that the son has a severe headache. "Carry him to his mother" (19).	"They will be divided: father against son and son against father" (53).
The mother says, "'I will run to the man of God and return. And he said, 'Why is it that you go to him today? It is not a new moon or a Sabbath.' But she said, 'Peace'" (22–23).	"Do you think that I have come to bring peace to the earth?" (51).
"Lead. Go. Do not hold back" (24).	"What stress I am under until it is completed" (50).
"'Is there peace with you? Or is there peace with your husband? Or is there peace with the boy?' She said (deceptively), 'There is peace'" (26).	"Do you think that I have come to bring peace to the earth?" (51).
"The Lord has hidden it from me and you and has not told it to me" (27).	"Why do you not know how to interpret the present time?" (56).
Elisha sends Gehazi, instead of going himself (29).	"And why do you not judge for yourself what is right?" (57).

Luke's Echoes of the Prophets Elijah and Elisha

Accused of deception, "Elisha arose and went after her" (30).	"When you go with your accuser" (58).
Elisha sends Gehazi on ahead to attempt to heal the boy by means of Elisha's staff (29–31).	"On the way make an effort to settle the case" (58).

4 Kgdms 4:38–44, countered by Luke 13:1–9

A toxic gourd added to a kettle of pottage (4:39).	Blood mingled with sacrifices (13:1).
"Death is in the kettle" (40).	Death is in the news (slaughtered Galileans; victims of structural collapse) (1–4).
A man brings firstfruit loaves and fruitcakes to the man of God (42).	A fig tree gives no fruit (6).
A servant objects to the reasonableness of the prophet's order to serve out a few loaves to feed a hundred people (43).	A gardener advises against the landowner's intention to cut down a fig tree (8–9).
"They had leftovers" (44).	The fig tree seems to need something extra (8–9).

4 Kgdms 5:1–19, imitated by Luke 13:10–17

"The man was a strong soldier who had become leprous" (5:1).	A woman had become crippled (13:11).
The king is indignant because they expect him to have healing power (6–7). Naaman is indignant because he does not receive a personal and dramatic healing (11–12).	A synagogue leader is indignant because Jesus heals on the wrong day (14).
"Wash seven times . . . and you will be clean" (10).	"You are set free from your ailment" (12).
"If the prophet spoke to you a great matter, would you not do it? But you would not do it because he said to you, 'Wash and be cleansed!'" (13). Argument from lesser to greater.	"You hypocrites! Does not each of you on the sabbath untie his ox . . . and lead it away to give it water?" (15). Argument from lesser to greater.

81

"He went and stood and said, 'Look, I know that there is no God in all the earth except in Israel'" (15).

"Immediately she stood up straight and began praising God" (13).

4 Kgdms 5:20—6:7, imitated by Luke 13:18-21

Without approval, Gehazi "takes" (5:23, 24, 26) silver and garments.	Someone "took" a spurious seed and sowed it (13:19).
"You took the garments, and olive yards, vineyards" (26). Gehazi's wants apparently are larger than just garments and silver.	"... in his garden. It grew and became a tree ...." (19).
"The place in which we reside ... is too small for us" (6:1). "Let us make for ourselves (a larger) place to live" (2).	A small seed grows into a large plant. A small lump of leaven (implied) suffuses three measures of flour. The kingdom grows from small to large surprisingly and invisibly (18–21).

4 Kgdms 6:8-23, imitated by Luke 13:22-30

Upon seeing an army surrounding Dothan, a servant cries, "O master, what will we do?" (6:15).	"Someone asked him, 'Lord, will only a few be saved?'" (13:23).
"He led them to Samaria" (19).	"Jesus ... made his way to Jerusalem" (22).
The Aramean troops "ate and drank" (23).	"We ate and drank with you" (26).
"He set before (the Aramean troops) a great dinner" in the Samaritan capital (23).	"People will come from east and west, from north and south, and will eat in the kingdom of God" (29).
"He sent (the Aramean troops) to their master" (23).	"Go away from me, all you evildoers!" (27).

4 Kgdms 6:24—7:2, imitated by Luke 13:31-35

Ben-Hadad of Aram besieges Samaria, attempting to starve it into submission (6:24–33).	"Herod wants to kill you" (13:31).
"Today ... tomorrow ... the next day" (28–29).	"Today, tomorrow, and the next day I must be on my way" (33).

Luke's Echoes of the Prophets Elijah and Elisha

The king of Israel "tore his garments" in lament over the plight of his city (30).	Jesus cries out in lament, "Jerusalem, Jerusalem . . ." (34).
The king threatens, "May God do to me and more, if the head of Elisha stands on him today" (31).	". . . the city that kills the prophets" (34).
"Elisha sat in his house, and the elders sat with him" (32).	"I desired to gather your children together as a hen gathers her brood under her wings" (34).
The king of Samaria "will see with the eyes, but (he) will not eat from it" (7:2).	"You will not see me until the time comes when you say, 'Blessed is the one who comes in the name of the Lord'" (35).

4 Kgdms 7:3-20, imitated by Luke 14:1-14

"The famine is in the city" (7:4).	"Jesus was going to the house of a leader of the Pharisees to eat a meal" (14:1).
"Four men were leprous beside the gate" (3).	"There was a man who had dropsy" (2).
The lepers consider whether they might live or die by the gate, or in the city, or in the army camp of Aram (4).	Jesus questions, "Is it lawful to cure people on the sabbath, or not?" (3).
A leper admits that they are not doing right in failing to report the empty camp. "This is a day of good tidings, and we remain silent" (9).	"If one of you has a child or an ox that has fallen into a well, will you not immediately pull it out on a sabbath day?" (5).
The king suspects that Aram is sitting in the fields so that, when Israel comes out to plunder the siege camp, Aram will jump up, capture them, and thus be able to enter the city of Samaria (12).	"When you are invited, go and sit down in the lowest place, so that when your host comes, he may say to you, 'Friend, move up higher'" (10).
The starving people of Samaria, including lepers, went out and plundered the siege camp (16).	"When you give a banquet, invite the poor, the crippled, the lame, and the blind" (13).

4 Kgdms 8:1–6, echoed by Luke 14:15–24

"Go . . . and live wherever you (can), because the Lord has decreed a famine in the land" (8:1).	"Blessed is anyone who will eat bread" (14:15).
At the end of the prophesied seven-year famine, a woman returns from sojourn to resume living in Israel (3).	"Someone gave a great dinner and invited many" (16).
"She went to cry to the king concerning her own house and concerning her own land" (3).	An invitee made an excuse to the dinner host: "I have bought a piece of land, and I must go out and see it" (18).
The king wants to be told "all the great things that Elisha did" (4), perhaps hearing that at the time of his call, Elisha was plowing behind twelve yoke of oxen.	"I have bought five yoke of oxen, and I am going to try them out" (19).
"The king gave her one eunuch, saying, (commandeer) 'all that was hers, the produce from the field from the day when she left the land until now'" (6).	"The master said to the slave, 'Go out into the roads and lanes, and compel people to come in'" (23).

4 Kgdms 8:7–24, imitated by Luke 14:25–35

"Elisha went to Damascus" (8:7).	Jesus was traveling (14:25).
"Hazael (representing Ben-hadad) went to meet him" (9).	"Whoever comes to me . . ." (26).
"Will I recover from this sickness?" "You will live by life . . . you will die by death" (9–10).	". . . and does not hate . . . life itself" (26).
Edom revolts and appoints a king. Joram of Judah mounts a chariot attack on them, but Edom's chariots overcome Joram's chariots (20–21).	"What king going out to wage war" will not "consider whether he is able . . . to oppose" the other king (31)?
"Edom has revolted . . . then Libnah revolted" (22).	You must "give up all your possessions" (33).

Luke's Echoes of the Prophets Elijah and Elisha

4 Kgdms 8:25—9:13, illustrated by Luke 15:1-10

Ahaziah of Judah joins evil-doing Joram of Israel to battle Hazael (8:28). Later, Ahaziah goes to visit the wounded Joram (29).	"This fellow welcomes sinners and eats with them" (15:2).
A messenger asks Jehu son of Jehoshaphat to step away from a meeting of military chiefs to receive the prophet's message (9:2, 5, 6).	A person will leave ninety-nine sheep to seek a lost one (4).
The military chiefs insist that Jehu not dissemble, but reveal the truth (11–12).	A person lights a lamp and searches the house carefully to find one lost coin (8).
"When they heard this they hurried, and each took his outer garment and placed it under him . . . , and they gave a signal by the horn and said, 'Jehu became king!'" (13).	"When she has found it, she calls together her friends and neighbors, saying 'Rejoice with me'" (9).

4 Kgdms 9:14-37, countered by Luke 15:11-32

"Jehu . . . conspired against Joram" (9:14).	A son demands his inheritance while his father is still living (15:11).
"The guard . . . saw the dust of Jehu when he was coming" (17).	"While he was still far off, his father saw him . . ." (20).
A rider "went to meet him" (18). A second rider "went to him" (19). Joram and Ahaziah "went out to meet Jehu" (21).	". . . and was filled with compassion; he ran and put his arms around him and kissed him" (20).
"How is there peace while the immorality of Jezebel" and her sorceries continue (22)?	"Father, I have sinned against heaven and before you" (21).
"Pick up and throw him on (Naboth's) plot" (26).	Put a robe on him, and a ring, and sandals (22).
Jehu called to those serving Jezebel. "Who are you? Come down with me. . . . Throw her down" (32–33).	"He called to one of the slaves and asked what was going on" (26).
"He went in and ate and drank" (34).	"He became angry and refused to go in" (28).

Kings, Deliverers, and Prophets in Luke's Journey Narrative

"'Bury (this cursed woman) because she is the daughter of a king.' They went out to bury her, but they did not find any part of her" except hands, feet, and skull (34–35).	"This brother of yours was dead and has come to life; he was lost and has been found" (32).

4 Kgdms 10:1–36, imitated by Luke 16:1–18

Ahab is dead, but his commanders, elders, and family guardians still control Samaria (10:1).	"There was a rich man who had a manager" (16:1).
"Jehu wrote (them) a document" (1–2). "He wrote to them a second document" (6).	The master summoned the manager (2).
"Whatever you say to us we will do" (5).	"What will I do?" (3) "I have decided what to do" (4).
King Ahaziah has seventy sons and forty-two brothers, and thus must be confident of preserving his dynasty (7, 14).	A manager fraudulently provides future lodging for himself by reducing two debt records, one by 50 percent and one by 20 percent (6–7).
"I am zealous for the Lord" (16).	Be "faithful" and "devoted" to God (11–13).
"Jehu acted . . . to destroy the servants of Baal" (19).	"What is prized by human beings is an abomination in the sight of God" (15).
"Summon to me all the prophets of Baal, all his servants, and his priests. Let no man be overlooked" (19).	"The good news of the kingdom of God is proclaimed and everyone tries to enter it by force" (16).
"Jehu removed Baal from out of Israel" (28).	"Anyone who divorces his wife and marries another commits adultery" (18).
Jehu continued the cult of the high places in Bethel and Dan, with their golden heifers (29, 31).	"Whoever marries a woman divorced from her husband commits adultery" (18).
"Jehu was not careful to walk in the law of the Lord God of Israel with his whole heart" (31).	"It is easier for heaven and earth to pass away, than for one stroke of a letter in the law to be dropped" (17).

Luke's Echoes of the Prophets Elijah and Elisha

4 Kgdms 11:1–16, suggested by Luke 16:19–31

In the following table, Luke's text echoes its LXX model less closely than most Lukan journey texts echo their model. Nevertheless, parallel sets of characters indicate we are indeed still accurately hearing the imitative resonance.

The *dramatis personae* at this place in both 4 Kingdoms and Luke feature four parallel sets of characters: an antagonist (Athaliah; the rich man), a protagonist (Jehoiada the priest; Abraham in heaven), a fragile hero (the boy Joash; poor and sore Lazarus), and the protagonist's helpers (temple guards; angels).

Further, the *setting* in the Lukan text reflects the setting in the 4 Kingdoms text. Fine purple linens and sumptuous table in Luke reflect royal privilege in 4 Kingdoms. The Lukan parable's gate where Lazarus lies imitates the OT back bedroom located far from the throne. The rich man's vision from Hades of Abraham and Lazarus in paradise parallels Athaliah distantly viewing the festal coronation of Joash to replace her. The fixed chasm in Luke 16:26 reflects the obstacle Athaliah faces: resolute coup-minded guards in 4 Kingdoms 11:10–15. Together these factors confirm that we are correctly considering Luke 16:19–31 to be an echo of 4 Kingdoms 11:1–16, even though the respective *plots* have little in common.

Athaliah grasps political control by slaughtering all heirs to the throne (11:1), and then she rules the land (3).	A rich man lived an opulent life (19).
An infant heir is hidden in a secluded bedroom and nurtured there (2–3).	A poor, sick man, Lazarus, lay hopefully at the rich man's gate (20–21).
The infant "was not destroyed" (2).	"The poor man died ..." (22).
Temple guards conspire with Jehoiada to bring seven-year-old Joash to the temple (4–12).	"... and was carried away by angels to be with Abraham" (22).
Athaliah sees newly crowned Joash in the temple with Jehoiada and a crowd of well-wishers (13–14).	In Hades, the dead rich man "looked up and saw Abraham far away with Lazarus by his side" (23).

"Ahaliah tore her garments and shouted" (14).	"He called out" (24).
Jehoiada warns, "The one who goes after her will be put to death . . . by the sword" (15).	He urges that warning be given to his five brothers lest they also come into torment (27-28).

4 Kgdms 11:17—12:16, echoed by Luke 17:1-10

A commitment to be "a people for the Lord" (11:17).	"His disciples" (17:1).
Baal worship endures perversely in Judah (18).	"Occasions for stumbling" persist (1).
"Joash was a son of seven years when he began to rule" (21).	Make sure you protect "little ones" from stumbling (2).
"Joash did what was right before the Lord. . . . However, the high places were not removed" (12:2-3).	"If the same person sins against you seven times a day, and turns back to you seven times and says, 'I repent,' you must forgive" (4).
The priests did not, as commanded, repair the house of the Lord (5-7).	"If you had faith," you could command a tree "and it would obey you" (6).
Both the repair job and donations for it are taken out of the hands of the priests (8).	Slaves do what they are told without expecting thanks or privilege in return (7-9).
Silver from sin offerings and guilt offerings, however, "belonged to the priests" (16).	"We have done only what we ought to have done" (10).

4 Kgdms 12:17-21, imitated by Luke 17:11

Luke's imitation in 17:11 of 4 Kingdoms 12:17 (shown in the table below) begs further comment. To reach the vicinity of Gath from Damascus or from elsewhere in Aram, Hazael's troops must have crossed the Jezreel Valley, the borderland between Galilee and Samaria. Either they came along a highway from the north, passed through Galilee itself, crossed the Jezreel Valley to Megiddo, and followed the Via Maris to Gath, or they rounded the Sea of Galilee on its east side, then descended along the Jordan River to Beth-shean, and thus west through Jezreel to Megiddo and beyond.

Luke's Echoes of the Prophets Elijah and Elisha

Either way, Hazael's troops were "going through the region between Samaria and Galilee" (Luke 12:17) with the further goal of attacking Jerusalem, the capital of Judah.

For his imitation of 4 Kingdoms 12:17 Luke drew from the Jesus tradition an account that located Jesus in "the region between Samaria and Galilee" as he made his way to Jerusalem. On the normally reasonable assumption that for Jesus' journey from Galilee to Jerusalem, any travel notices should be geographically sequential, commentators and other Bible students puzzle over the anomaly that Jesus remains so far north so late in his southward journey to Jerusalem.

In our study, however, we discover and follow Luke's systematic parallels of text from 3 and 4 Kingdoms. On the assumption that Luke selects texts from the Jesus tradition *for the sake of paralleling* 3 and 4 Kingdoms material, Luke 17:11 is a particularly clear example of Luke picking an appropriate text to echo 4 Kingdoms 12:17.

"Hazael . . . set his face to go against Jerusalem" (12:17).	"On the way to Jerusalem" (17:11).
"Hazael, king of Aram, came up and made war at Gath" (17).	"Jesus was going through the region between Samaria and Galilee" (11).

4 Kgdms 13:1-13, imitated by Luke 17:12-19

"Jehoahaz . . . became king in Samaria" (13:1).	A Samaritan leper approaches Jesus (17:12, 16).
"Jehoahaz prayed to the face of the Lord," (4) because of heavy oppression by Aram.	He (and others) call out, "Jesus, master, have mercy on us! (13).
"The Lord gave salvation (*sōtērian*) for Israel" (5).	"Your faith has made you well (*sesōken*)" (19).
No Samaritan army was left from war "except fifty . . . , ten . . . , and ten thousand . . ." (7).	"Was none of them found to return . . . except this foreigner?" (18).

Kings, Deliverers, and Prophets in Luke's Journey Narrative

4 Kingdoms 13:14—14:22, pictured by Luke 17:20-37

The historian reports the death of Elisha in 4 Kingdoms 13:14–21, but Elisha's death does not bring this phase of Luke's imitative project to a close.

Joash wants to know if Israel will be saved from Aram (13:14–19).	"Jesus was asked by the Pharisees when the kingdom of God was coming" (17:20).
"Look!" (*idou*): when a corpse touched Elisha's bones, the corpse revived and stood up (21).	Do not pay attention when they say, "Look!" (*idou*; 21 [2x], 23 [2x])
"The Lord did not want to utterly destroy (Israel)" (23).	"In the days of Noah.... The flood came and destroyed all of them" (26–27). "In the days of Lot... it rained fire and sulphur from heaven and destroyed all of them" (28–29).
"It happened when the kingdom strengthened in his hand" (14:5).	"The kingdom of God is not coming with things that can be observed" (20).
Sons "shall die for (their own) sins" (14:6).	The Son of Man "must endure much suffering and be rejected by this generation" (24–25) before he dies for the sins of humanity.
"Give your daughter to my son for a wife" (14:9).	"They were... marrying and being given in marriage" (27).
"Remain in your house" (10).	"Anyone on the housetop who has belongings in the house must not come down to take them away" (31).
Joash, king of Israel, "and Amaziah, king of Judah, looked at each other" (11). Then Israel defeated Judah (12).	"There will be two in one bed; one will be taken and the other left" (34).
Amaziah "fled to Lachish, and they sent after him to Lachish and killed him there" (19).	"'Where, Lord?' He said to them, 'Where the corpse is, there the vultures will gather'" (37).

Greek New Testaments and modern translations of Luke leave out 17:36, mentioning it instead in a footnote or apparatus. The subordinated text continues the concept, syntax, and vocabulary of

Luke's Echoes of the Prophets Elijah and Elisha

Luke 17:34–35, except that the imagined location of a third pair of people is "in the field," rather than "in one bed" or "grinding meal together." Two actors "in the field" parallels an LXX model that describes two kings and their armies staring one another down across a bit of land. Further, two actors "in one bed" is consonant with the historic and theological tie between Israel and Judah. The manuscripts offering "in the field," however, come to light only in the sixth century CE.

4 Kgdms 14:23–29, countered by Luke 18:1–8

"The Lord saw the humiliation of Israel, very bitter, and those constrained were few, exhausted and in want, and Israel had no helper" (14:26).	An ungodly and dispassionate local judge does not want to umpire property complaints (18:2). A widow "kept coming to him and saying, 'Grant me justice against my opponent'" (3).
"The Lord said he would not wipe out the seed of Israel from beneath heaven" (27).	"He said to himself, 'Though I have no fear of God and no respect for anyone, yet because this widow keeps bothering me, I will grant her justice" (4–5).
"He saved them from the hand of Jeroboam the son of Joash" (27).	"Will not God grant justice to his chosen ones who cry to him day and night?" (7). "I tell you, he will quickly grant justice to them" (8).

4 Kgdms 15:1–7, imitated by Luke 18:9–14

Azariah "did what was right in the eyes of the Lord" (15:3).	Some "trusted in themselves that they were righteous" (18:9).
Due to lifelong leprosy, King Azariah lived in quarantine in a separate house. His son, Jonathan, managed the house and judged Israel (1–5).	"Two men went up to the temple to pray" (10).
Jonathan, the son, is healthy, but Azariah, the king (and therefore a gatherer of revenue) is a leper (5).	"God, I thank you that I am not like other people: thieves, rogues, adulterers, or even like this tax collector" (11).
Azariah "was king in a separate house" (5).	The tax collector stood far off (13).

Azariah failed to "remove the high places" (4).	"God, be merciful to me, a sinner" (13).
Azariah "was king in a separate house" (5).	"This man went down to his home justified" (14).
Azariah's deeds, not his son Jonathan's deeds, were written in the "deeds for the annals for the kings of Judah" (6).	"All who exalt themselves will be humbled, but all who humble themselves will be exalted" (14).

4 Kgdms 15:8-12, imitated by Luke 18:15-17

"Your sons to the fourth generation" (15:12).	"Let the little children come to me . . ." (8:16).
"The word of the Lord . . . And it was so" (12).	". . . and do not stop them; for it is to such as these that . . ." (16).
"They will sit on the throne of Israel" (12).	". . . the kingdom of God belongs" (16).

4 Kgdms 15:13-38, rendered by Luke 18:18-30

"Shallum . . . reigned a day in Samaria" (15:13).	"A certain ruler asked him . . . 'What must I do to inherit eternal life?'" (18:18).
Menahem "ripped open women who were pregnant" (16).	"You shall not murder" (20).
"Menahem gave Pul a thousand talents of silver" (19).	"Sell all that you own and distribute the money" (22).
"Menahem exacted the silver . . . against all who were strong in wealth" (20).	"He was very rich" (23).
Argob and Arieh were murdered outside of the king's house while attending King Pekehiah (25).	"We have left our homes and followed you" (28).

4 Kgdms 16:1-20, imitated by Luke 18:31—19:10

The right side of the table below surveys two Lukan texts (18:35-43; 19:1-10) that echo only one text in 4 Kingdoms (16:7-20). Such an analysis of the parallels is not my contrivance to make it work. The two Lukan texts in question are a single unit of discourse

Luke's Echoes of the Prophets Elijah and Elisha

in Luke's journey narrative, having much in common lexically and expressing quite similar responses to Jesus. Lexical commonalities include visiting Jericho (18:35; 19:1), a man unable to see Jesus (18:35–37; 19:3–4), a hindering crowd (18:36–39; 19:3), addressing Jesus as "Lord" (18:41; 19:8), and an emotionally engaged crowd (18:43; 19:7). In their encounters with Jesus, the two men become zealous disciples (18:43; 19:8–9). For the 4 Kingdoms/Luke parallel we are tracing, it is entirely appropriate that these Lukan "fraternal twin" episodes share the same "parent" text in 4 Kingdoms.

King Ahaz of Judah "carried (sacrificed) his son . . ." (16:3).	"Everything that is written about the Son of Man . . . will be accomplished" (18:31).
". . . through fire and the abominations . . ." (3).	Mocked, insulted, flogged, killed (32–33).
". . . of the nations (*tōn ethnōn*)" (3).	"He will be handed over to the Gentiles (*tois ethnesin*)" (32).
Rezin of Aram and Pekah of Israel "went up to Jerusalem (against Ahaz) for battle" (5).	"We are going up to Jerusalem" (31).
"They laid siege against Ahaz, but they were not able to fight" (5).	"They understood nothing about all these things; . . . they did not grasp what was said" (34).
Messengers tell Tiglath-Pileser that Aram and Israel "are rising up against" Ahaz (7).	Members of the crowd tell the blind man that "Jesus of Nazareth is passing by" (36–37).
"The king of Assyria heard him" (9) and responded.	Jesus hears and says, "What do you want me to do for you?" (40).
King Ahaz "saw the altar" (10) and then "saw" Uriah's copy of the Aramean altar (12).	"Let me see again" (41).
On the altar, you will sacrifice the offerings "of all the people (*pantos tou laou*)" (15).	"All the people (*pas ho laos*) . . . praised God" (43).
The historian names "Uriah the priest" four times (10, 11, 15, 16).	"A man was there named Zacchaeus; he was a chief tax collector and was rich" (19:2). "Zacchaeus, hurry" (5). "Zacchaeus stood there" (8).

Ahaz "went up (*anebē*)" on the altar (12).	Zacchaeus "climbed (*anebē*) a sycamore tree" (4).
Ahaz made arrangements to offer "burnt offering" (13, 15 [4x]) and "drink offering" (13, 15) to the Lord.	Zacchaeus provides refreshment for Jesus (5–7).
"Uriah the priest did according to all, as much as King Ahaz commanded him" (16).	"Half of my possessions, Lord, I will give to the poor; and if I have defrauded anyone of anything, I will pay back four times as much" (8).

4 Kgdms 17:1–6, imitated by Luke 19:11–27

After Hoshea became king in Samaria, Shalmaneser of Assyria attacked and subjugated Hoshea, who "returned manach" (tribute) to Shalmaneser (probably as a vassal king) (17:1–3).	"A nobleman went to a distant country to get royal power for himself and then return" (19:12).
"Hoshea became a slave" to Shalmaneser (3).	The nobleman "summoned ten of his slaves" (13).
Hoshea sought to subvert Shalmaneser's grasp on Israel. "He sent messengers to Zoar, king of Egypt" (4).	"Citizens of his country hated (the nobleman) and sent a delegation . . . saying, 'We do not want this man to rule over us'" (14).
"The king of Assyria found wrongdoing in Hoshea" (4), who had sought deliverance from bitter subjugation to Assyria.	The king said to the slave, "You wicked slave! You knew, did you, that I was a harsh man, taking what I did not deposit and reaping what I did not sow?" (22).

4 Kgdms 17:7–12, imitated by Luke 19:28–44

"Their Lord God, who led them up from the land of Egypt" (17:7).	"He went on ahead, going up to Jerusalem" (19:28).
"The sons of Israel clothed their words" (9).	The disciples threw "their cloaks on the colt . . ." (35). "People kept spreading their cloaks on the road" (36).

Luke's Echoes of the Prophets Elijah and Elisha

"They built for themselves high places in all their cities, from the guards' tower to the fortified city" (9).

"Your enemies will set up ramparts around you and surround you" (43).

Luke 13:34-35 serves both as an essential middle block of journey text and as a journey bookend text. In the bookend role, Luke 13:34-35 imitates a part of 4 Kingdoms coming just before the fall of the Northern Israelite Kingdom under the onslaught of Assyria.[7]

4 Kgdms 17:13-23, imitated by Luke 13:34-35

"The Lord warned Israel and Judah through the hand of all his prophets and all the word of seers ... '(Warnings) that I sent to them by the hand of my servants the prophets'" (17:13).

"Jerusalem, Jerusalem, the city that kills the prophets and stones those who are sent to it" (13:34).

"They did not listen, but they hardened their back more than the back of their fathers" (14).

"You were not willing" (34).

"There was nothing left except the tribe of Judah alone" (18). "Israel was removed from the house of David" (21).

"Your house is left (desolate, forsaken) to you" (35).

With that tragedy and its echoing lament, we conclude our display of echoes (imitations, parallels, reflections) of the stories of key OT leaders that Luke parallels in ten chapters of the Third Gospel. In our final chapter, we will clarify the purpose of Luke's complex echoing journey narrative.

---

7. See Appendix 1.

> Master, God! Oh, please, look on me again,
> Oh, please, give strength yet once more.
>
> JUDG 16:28 (*MSG*)

> Master, I want to see again.
>
> LUKE 18:41 (*MSG*)

6

The Purpose of Luke's Journey Narrative

LUKE COMPILES AND EDITS a unique Galilee-to-Jerusalem journey narrative in which Jesus' words and acts reflect David's odyssey to Israel's kingship. Further, all episodes of the same Lukan journey narrative parallel the stories of Moses and the judges contending with military and spiritual threats facing Israel. And more, Luke's ten-chapter account of Jesus' journey to Jerusalem echoes accounts of both Elijah and Elisha speaking God's word to Israel. The words and actions of Jesus in Luke 9:51—19:44 parallel persons and events in the LXX texts of Numbers 10:11—36:13, Judges 1:1—21:25, 1 Kingdoms 19:11—2 Kingdoms 6:23, and 3 Kingdoms 19:1—4 Kingdoms 25:21. What kind of a composition can simultaneously parallel and echo three other stories?[1] What is Luke's journey narrative? What is its purpose? Let us eliminate some possible answers.

---

1. First and Second Kgdms and 3–4 Kgdms each form one account, divided in two by the limitations of scroll length. Luke treats Num 10:11—36:13, together with Judg 1:1—21:25, as one account of God's deliverers contending with nations opposing Israel.

The Purpose of Luke's Journey Narrative

REWRITTEN SCRIPTURE

Most obviously, Luke's journey narrative is not rewritten Scripture. The books of the Chronicles, for example, retell a single story of Israel from 1 Samuel 31 through 2 Kings 25. Josephus rewrites the Old Testament for the Roman public in his *Antiquities of the Jews*. Authors rewrite Scripture to move the source material in a new interpretive direction by selecting and deselecting certain episodes of the source material, by supplementing, and by editing and narrating the revised story. In a revised story one can recognize a version of the original story (Chronicles looks like Samuels and Kings). Almost all of Luke 9:51—19:44, however, is teaching, not plot development in the manner of Luke's models. In consequence, one does not recognize the *stories* of Moses, the judges, David, Elijah, and Elisha in Luke's journey narrative. Luke does not attempt to retell, reframe, popularize, summarize, or reinterpret any of the OT stories that he engages in Luke 9–19.

COMMENTARY

Luke does not assemble a commentary on the doings of Moses, of the judges, of David, or of Elijah and Elisha, even though the journey narrative is replete with Jesus' teaching.[2] One can indeed discern what appears to be fragmentary theological comment in lines of Jesus' teaching compared to snippets of text in parallel locations in our three OT stories. For example, Jesus asks, "Do you thank the slave for doing what was commanded?" (Luke 17:9), and in the parallel Judges text, Israel clamors for successful judge Gideon to be awarded de facto kingship over them (Judg 8:22). Jesus' rhetorical question could be taken as confirmation of Gideon's answer: "I will not rule . . . the Lord will rule" (8:23).

Another example concerns Jesus' teaching, "No one knows . . . who the Father is except the Son and anyone to whom the Son chooses to reveal him" (Luke 10:22). In the parallel location

---

2. Luke describes only a few actions of Jesus, along with many circumstantial clauses describing where, when, and with whom conversations and teaching take place.

in 1 Kingdoms 20, Jonathan, son of King Saul, confidently assures David that Jonathan knows fully what Saul is thinking (1 Kgdms 20:2). In this case, Jesus could be taken to teach regarding Saul and Jonathan that what is true in the heavenly realm (the Son knows the Father) could also be true in the earthly realm (Jonathan thinks he knows the mind of Saul). One can find numerous comments of Jesus among parallel Luke-to-OT texts potentially affirming, denying, or correcting OT characters and events. In a few places, an entire episode from Luke 9–19 offers a series of possible comments on an entire episode of OT text.[3]

Such possible interpretive connections, however, are usually brief, disconnected, atomistic. Even when a Lukan episode seems to offer multiple interpretive openings for an entire OT episode, the possible expositions do not connect into an interpretive discourse: they prove to be a miscellany, like marbles in a jar. Numerous and sequentially parallel themes, scenes, and wording between Luke and OT stories tell us that we are on to something remarkable, but they do not amount to theological commentary.

Since each Lukan journey teaching episode parallels as many as three OT passages concurrently, none of these Lukan episodes could provide a commentary on only one of the three OT passages. Often, a sentence in Luke 9:51—19:44 echoes words of all three OT models, or echoes two of the three OT models. Rarely in the journey narrative do Luke's sentences reflect content from only one of the three OT models. Luke's intermixture of allusions to three OT models *does not allow even the possibility of sustained meaningful commentary*. Luke does not assemble a commentary by Jesus on the doings of Moses, of the judges, of David, or of Elijah and Elisha.

GRECO-ROMAN IMITATION

Nor does Luke write his journey narrative as Greco-Roman imitation, even though he may have been educated in an imitative literary culture. In the ancient Greek and Roman cultural world,

---

3. See, for example, the table on pages 19–20, showing that Luke 12:1–12 parallels an entire episode in 1 Kgdms 24.

The Purpose of Luke's Journey Narrative

advanced students were taught to imitate models from great Greek classics in various genres. A classically trained writer could quote certain great authors from memory and mimic or readily allude to their compositions. Homer stood alone as the highest model for imitation. After him, as a second tier, literary authorities of the era urged emulation of such authors as Aeschylus, Sophocles, Euripides, Menander, Herodotus, Thucydides, Xenophon, Plato, and a short list of others.[4] Ambitious and articulate writers often sought to emulate and rival classic authors and works, trying to surpass the achievements and reputations of revered Greek authors.

As a highly literate Christian author, Luke possibly had typical advanced training for his time. And it is likely that Luke was very familiar with great classical journeys such as Homer's *Odyssey* and Virgil's *Aeneid*, passages of which he would have been able to echo in Jesus' journey. But he does not do so: he echoes four biblical accounts. Luke finds his journey models in Israel's Scriptures, not in Greek classics.

Nor does Luke exhibit intent to rival any of his sources.[5] The evangelist never puts forward his own name as an exalted rival author. When naming the recipient of his narrative (Theophilus), Luke does not name himself (1:1-4), and Luke remains unnamed elsewhere in the Third Gospel.[6] The evangelist remains a proponent of Jesus of Nazareth, not a proponent of himself or of the classical heritage.

SOMETHING REMARKABLE

Luke's journey narrative is not rewritten Scripture, nor a commentary, nor a Greco-Roman imitation. The teaching (and a few actions) of Jesus in Luke 9:51—19:44 parallels textual details in the LXX of Numbers 10:11—36:13, Judges 1:1—21:25, 1 Kingdoms

---

4. See Dupertuis, "Writing and Imitation," 7-8, for a general description of imitation.

5. See Brodie, "Departure for Jerusalem," 98, and MacDonald, *Luke and Virgil*, 13, for the culture of rivalry.

6. Luke's name became attached to the narrative several decades after it began circulating (see Green, *Gospel of Luke*, 20-21).

Kings, Deliverers, and Prophets in Luke's Journey Narrative

19:11—2 Kingdoms 6:23, and 3 Kingdoms 19:1—4 Kingdoms 25:21. Just as Luke's "Gospel" as a whole (and Luke-Acts as a whole) do not readily fit ancient (or modern) classifications of religious literature, so also Luke's journey narrative has no recognizable literary or theological predecessor.

While we cannot successfully classify these central chapters of Luke, we can detect theological motivation for them. Luke's journey episodes confirm what Luke proclaims elsewhere in his narrative: that Jesus is the eschatological Deliverer, the eschatological King, and the eschatological Prophet.

Sustained thematic parallels of Moses and the judges to Jesus in Luke 9:51—19:44 press the reader of Luke to make a more generalized connection between the deliverers and Jesus: he is the great, final, eschatological Deliverer. In the prophetic words of Zechariah,

> Blessed be the Lord God of Israel,
> for he has looked favorably on his people and redeemed them.
> He has raised up a mighty savior for us in the house of David,
> As he spoke through the mouth of his holy prophets of old,
> that we would be saved from our enemies and from the hand of all who hate us.
> Thus he has shown the mercy promised to our ancestors,
> and has remembered his holy covenant,
> the oath that he swore to our ancestor Abraham,
> to grant us that we, being rescued from the hands of our enemies,
> might serve him without fear, in holiness and righteousness
> before him all our days. (Luke 1:68–75)

Zechariah's child was not the "mighty savior" (*keras sōtērias*, 69, cf. 3:16), but would "go before" him (1:17; 3:16). The mighty Savior-Deliverer was Jesus.

Likewise, by parallel sequences of themes, Jesus' journey parallels David's odyssey: fleeing from the king, becoming king, and then welcoming the King of Kings. These striking thematic and topical parallels push the reader of Luke to remember the announcement of the angel Gabriel, "You will conceive in your womb and bear a son, and you will name him Jesus. He will be great and will be called the Son of the Most High, and the Lord God will give to him the throne of his ancestor David. He will reign over the

The Purpose of Luke's Journey Narrative

house of Jacob forever, and of his kingdom there will be no end" (Luke 1:31-33), and to remember a further angelic announcement, "To you is born this day in the city of David a Savior, who is the Messiah, the Lord" (2:11; cf. 9:20). The Lukan journey of the eschatological King echoes the odyssey of David and recalls announcements of the Messiah's advent.[7]

Finally, certain expressions in episodes making up Jesus' journey in Luke thematically and sequentially match words and themes in the careers of Elijah, Elisha, and of other prophets in 3 Kingdoms 19:1—4 Kingdoms 17:23. Such prominent parallels of Jesus' teaching to OT prophetic ministries urge Luke's reader to recall that Jesus, early in his ministry, made it clear that

> The Spirit of the Lord is upon me,
> because he has anointed me
> to bring good news to the poor.
> He has sent me to proclaim release to the captives
> and recovery of sight to the blind,
> to let the oppressed go free,
> to proclaim the year of the Lord's favor. (4:18-19; cf. 4:21)

Jesus is the prophet who manifests Isaiah's vision of a great prophet proclaiming hope and restoration to Israel (Isa 60:1-2, cited by Jesus in Luke 4:18). Further, and provocatively for our thesis, Jesus claims the precedent of Elijah and Elisha for his own ministry (4:22-27).[8] Nor is a connection between Jesus and Elijah lost on the crowd that observes Jesus raise a young man from the dead and give him back alive to his mother (7:14-16, cf. 3 Kgdms 17:17-24). The Great Prophet has come in the person of Jesus.

Jesus Christ is God's Prophet, God's King, and God's Deliverer of the last day. Parallels of Luke 9-19 to Numbers and Judges confirm what Zechariah proclaims (Luke 1:68-75): that God raises up a mighty Savior-Deliverer for Israel. Correspondences between David's odyssey to the throne and the Lukan journey attest by

---

7. The Third Gospel, outside of the travel narrative, presents Jesus as the eschatological deliverer (Luke 4:16-27; 7:16), the eschatological prophet (2:29-35; 4:17-30; 4:42—5:1; 7:16), and the eschatological king (1:32-33; 2:11; 9:20; 21:25-28; 22:67-69).

8. See Green, *Gospel of Luke*, 217.

reflections that Jesus is the very King that angels proclaimed to Mary and to the shepherds. Persistent thematic similarities between prophetic ministry to the Northern Kingdom of Israel and Jesus' words and actions in Luke 9:51—19:44 give secondary testimony by echoes that Jesus is the promised Great Prophet.

Luke's narrative is a prodigious journey narrative indeed, from the hand of a remarkable editor-compiler-narrator. The writer and his text go into uncharted literary territory. Triple-voiced echoes of narrative resound in one narrative, yielding one credible story quite unlike the three models. Luke adeptly discovers and selects episodes from the gospel tradition that connect in numerous ways concurrently back to three OT stories. He edits and compiles text to subtly reveal echoes of his models. In so doing, Luke confirms divine proclamations recounted earlier in his Gospel that the Deliverer, the Prophet, and the King have come in the person of Jesus Christ.

Appendix 1

The Roles of Luke 13:31–35

LUKE EMPLOYS LUKE 13:31–35 in two ways for the journey's echoes of the king, of the deliverers, and of the prophets.

First, the evangelist selects 13:31–35 from the tradition and places the text in the middle of the journey narrative to echo (reflect, imitate, parallel) texts in the middle of his models. Accordingly, Luke 13:31–35, by one set of its features, echoes 1 Kingdoms 31:1—2 Kingdoms 1:27; by another set of its features Luke 13:31–35 echoes Numbers 33:1–49 together with Judges 1:1–21; and by another set of its features it echoes 4 Kingdoms 6:24—7:2. Luke echoes the middles of three OT stories by the middle passage of his journey narrative.

The Lukan journey narrative, however, has a *nonlinear feature*. Luke 13:31–33 and 34–35 are written in the middle of the journey, but are also texts to be read (projected, visualized) as the beginning of the beginning of the narrative (13:31–33 ahead of 9:51) and the beginning of the end of the narrative (13:34–35 ahead of 19:42).[1] These middle-journey texts, when projected to the outer ends of the journey narrative, also participate at those outer locations in Luke's echoing project.

---

1. Luke 13:31–33 provides a satisfying immediate context for Jesus' departure toward Jerusalem, while Luke 13:34–35 provides the first half of a formal ritual lament that concludes in 19:42–44. See more detail in Chadwick, *Both Here and There*, 144–50.

Appendix 1

Accordingly, the second way that Luke employs 13:31-33 and 34-35 is in connection with the Lukan journey's beginning and end. Luke 13:31-33 echoes the beginnings of OT stories, and 13:34-35 echoes the endings of OT stories. For Luke's beginning echoes, certain features of 13:31-33 combine with certain features in Luke 9 to echo features of each of the three OT stories. The table below indicates the extents of model and echo in story beginnings.

Luke 13:31-33 and 9:51-56		1 Kgdms 19:11-18
Luke 13:31-33 and 9:51-62	echoes:	Num 10:11—11:3
Luke 13:31-33 and 9:51-60		3 Kgdms 19:1-14

When Luke echoes the ends of OT stories, certain features of 13:34-35 combine with certain features of 19:28-44 to form each echo. The following table lists the extent of OT models that are echoed by combining features of 13:34-35 and 19:28-44.

	Judg 19:1—21:25
Luke 13:34-35 and 19:28-44 echo:	2 Kgdms 6:1-23
	4 Kgdms 17:7-23

In this book's exploration of echoes of the OT in the Lukan journey, we identify Luke 13:31-33 and 34-35 as texts echoing the beginning and end of three OT stories, as well as texts echoing middle passages of those stories.

Appendix 2

Richard Hays and *Echoes of Scripture in the Gospels*

In 2016, Richard B. Hays brought out *Echoes of Scripture in the Gospels*, a work describing ways in which the Gospels connect their messages to the OT. Hays describes how Gospel writers put forward lengthy narratives in complex prose textures that resound with echoes of OT events and persons. Regarding echoes of events and persons in Luke's Gospel, Hays states:

> The opening two chapters of [Luke] create a vivid expectation of the fulfillment of scriptural promise, and the concluding resurrection appearance stories assert forthrightly that Moses and the Prophets and the Psalms are somehow fulfilled in Jesus (Luke 24:25–27,44–47). Yet in between these signposts, the narrative offers, for the most part, only elusive hints and reminiscences of Old Testament precursors. Luke "ripples with intertextuality" because it constantly folds Old Testament textual patterns into its story. The effect of this narrative technique is to lure us into the work of close, retrospectively alert reading, seeking to discern and interpret the intertextual clues woven into the fabric of the story.[1]

The textual territory between Hays's signposts in Luke includes, at the most central location, a journey of Jesus and the

---

1. Hays, *Echoes of Scripture*, 193.

Appendix 2

disciples from Galilee to Jerusalem (9:51—19:44). This is the biblical account for which we attempt to do "retrospectively alert reading, seeking to discern and interpret the intertextual clues woven into the fabric of the story."

Our retrospective reading of 1 and 2 Samuel, for example, finds numerous thematic clues of convergence with Luke's journey narrative, clues such as: Luke has "Lend me three loaves" (11:5) and 1 Samuel has "Give me five loaves of bread" (21:3). In Luke, Jesus tells a parable about a rich fool (12:13–27), while 1 Samuel narrates the story of Nabal, a rich fool (25:2–17). Jesus laments (Luke 13:34–35) and David laments (2 Sam 1:17–27). Jesus proclaims that the Son of Man "must endure much suffering and be rejected by this generation" (Luke 17:25), while in 2 Samuel, David grieves that "wicked men have killed a righteous man" (4:11). In Luke, Jesus tells his disciples to stop hindering little children being brought to him, "for it is to such as these that the kingdom of God belongs" (18:16). Analogously, David fills his royal home with many children born to him (2 Sam 5:11–15). And finally, like Jesus riding into Jerusalem on an unused colt (Luke 19:35–38), the ark of God travels toward Jerusalem on a new cart (2 Sam 6:1–5).

Two observations readily emerge from these intertextual clues. First, such clues in 1–2 Samuel are numerous. I have listed only six in the paragraph above, but our chapter 2 provides many more. Second, these intertextual clues line up in parallel sequence with Luke's journey narrative. When we compare Jesus' journey to Jerusalem (Luke 9:51—19:44) to David's odyssey toward the throne of Israel (1 Sam 19:11—2 Sam 6:23), clues in the Gospel echo clues in OT text in parallel sequence.

But here we need to interact with Hays's assessment of sequences among intertextual clues in Luke's Gospel:

> But it is not Luke's style to develop sustained sequences in which the patterns coincide and run parallel; rather, almost as soon as we recognize one such narrative convergence, the moment has passed, and a different image

appears on the backdrop, perhaps suggesting an entirely different set of linkages.[2]

In Lukan gospel texts, allusions to the OT are dense or "kaleidoscopic."[3] A single Gospel scene may evoke two, three, or more OT stories. The next Lukan sentence or the next Lukan scene may echo a considerably different OT scene or collection of them. Yet we also find that the Lukan journey narrative persistently echoes David's odyssey in successive Gospel episodes, frequently in unexpected echoic ways.[4] Such echoes resound again and again, OT story and Gospel story keeping pace with one another. Luke does indeed develop three sustained sequences in which patterns coincide and run parallel with OT texts.

These three narrative echoes are not heard readily for at least two reasons. Many or most of these echoes do not ring with specifically theological language, but with everyday things, events, and experiences, such as "manure" or "rich man." Thus, in the journey narrative Luke mostly assembles *literary echoes*, not primarily theological ones. If an interpreter strains to hear theological echoes only, she will not hear many. Second, Luke does not so much assemble Gospel episodes to give concentrated echoes of iconic OT scenes as he does drawn-out reverberations across entire acts in the OT drama of God: David's odyssey to the throne, deeds of God's flawed deliverers, and the ministry of the northern prophets. In the journey narrative, Luke develops echoic convergences to OT narrative arcs. The awaited king has come, God's deliverer has arisen, God's prophet has spoken.

---

2. Hays, *Echoes of Scripture*, 193.
3. Hays, *Echoes of Scripture*, 193.
4. We give David's odyssey as the example here, but the same point can be made regarding echoes ringing between the Lukan journey and: Moses as God's deliverer in Numbers, the deliverers of Judges, Elijah/Elisha in 1 and 2 Kings.

Bibliography

Block, Daniel I. *Judges/Ruth*. New American Commentary 6. Nashville: B&H, 1999.
Brodie, Thomas L. "The Departure for Jerusalem (Luke 9,51–56) as a Rhetorical Imitation of Elijah's Departure for the Jordan (2 Kgs 1,1—2,6)." *Biblica* 70 (1989) 96–109.
Chadwick, Dennis W. *Both Here and There: Studies in Concentric Parallelism in the Gospel of Luke*. Eugene, OR: Wipf & Stock, 2018.
Dupertuis, Rubén R. "Writing and Imitation: Greek Education in the Greco-Roman World." *Forum* 1:1 (2007) 3–8.
Fitzmyer, Joseph A. *The Gospel According to Luke I–IX*. The Anchor Bible. New York: Doubleday, 1981.
———. *The Gospel According to Luke X–XXIV*. The Anchor Bible. New York: Doubleday, 1985.
Green, Joel. *The Gospel of Luke*. Grand Rapids: Eerdmans, 1997.
Hays, Richard B. *Echoes of Scripture in the Gospels*. Waco, TX: Baylor University Press, 2016.
Jobes, Karen H., and Moisés Silva. *Invitation to the Septuagint*. 2nd ed. Grand Rapids: Baker Academic, 2015.
Kohlenberger, John R. *The NIV Triglot Old Testament*. Grand Rapids: Zondervan, 1981.
MacDonald, Dennis R. *Luke and Virgil: Imitations of Classic Greek Literature*. The New Testament and Greek Literature 2. Lanham, MD: Rowman & Littlefield, 2015.
Milgrom, Jacob. *Numbers: The Traditional Hebrew Text with the New JPS Translation*. JPS Torah Commentary. Philadelphia: Jewish Publication Society, 1990.
Miura, Yuzuru. *David in Luke-Acts: His Portrayal in Light of Early Judaism*. Tübingen: Mohr Siebeck, 2007.
Moessner, David P. *Lord of the Banquet: The Literary and Theological Significance of the Lukan Travel Narrative*. Minneapolis: Augsburg Fortress, 1989.
Penner, Ken M., ed. *The Lexham English Septuagint*. Bellingham, WA: Lexham, 2019.

Bibliography

Swete, Henry B. *The Old Testament in Greek*. Cambridge: Cambridge University Press, 1887.

Tsumura, David Toshio. *The First Book of Samuel*. New International Commentary on the Old Testament 9. Grand Rapids: Eerdmans, 2007.

———. *The Second Book of Samuel*. New International Commentary on the Old Testament 10. Grand Rapids: Eerdmans, 2019.

Wenham, Gordon J. *Numbers*. Tyndale Old Testament Commentaries. Leicester: Inter-Varsity, 1981.

Whitmarsh, Tim. *Greek Literature and the Roman Empire: The Politics of Imitation*. Oxford: Oxford University Press, 2001.

Wiseman, Donald J. *1 and 2 Kings*. Tyndale Old Testament Commentaries 9. Downers Grove, IL: InterVarsity, 1993.

Wright, Matthew. "The Tragedian as Critic: Euripides and Early Greek Poetics." *Journal of Hellenic Studies* 130 (2010) 165–84. https://www.jstor.org/stable/41722538

Wright, N. T. *The New Testament and the People of God*. Minneapolis: Fortress, 1992.

www.ingramcontent.com/pod-product-compliance
Lightning Source LLC
Chambersburg PA
CBHW070928160426
43193CB00011B/1611